richard jackson's
CONTAINER
GARDENING

richard jackson's
CONTAINER
GARDENING

How to grow wonderful pots, hanging baskets and window boxes

rj

Jigsaw Marketing & Media
PO Box 703
Bucks HP6 9BX

www.richardjacksonsgarden.co.uk

First published in the UK in 2013 by
Jigsaw Marketing & Media Ltd.

First edition

Design & Editorial **Arthur Brown**
Production **Peter Cooling**
Index **Venessa Bird**

ISBN 978-0-9574117-0-8

A CIP catalogue record for this book is
avilable from the British Library.

Typeset in Cochin, Binny Old Style
and Frutiger.

Printed and bound in China through
Asia Pacific Offset.

Contents

Introduction

I was helping stage my very first Chelsea Flower Show exhibit when it suddenly dawned on me just how exciting container gardening could be. I was part of a team on the Hillier Nurseries stand and we'd just unloaded four lorry loads of plants. All of them, from huge trees to tiny alpines, were grown in pots. Over the course of three days we gradually carried each plant, the biggest first and the smallest last, into position to create the most wonderful garden full of colour, beauty and fragrance. I was chuffed to bits when our container grown garden was then awarded the highest honour, the coveted Royal Horticultural Society gold medal.

At the end of the show, the garden was dismantled and all the plants were transported back to the nursery where they were carefully cared for over the season until the following Chelsea. When I helped unload the lorries that year, it was just like meeting old friends again. To my delight, there were the very same pot grown wisterias, azaleas and crab apple trees – all looking slightly bigger and even more beautiful.

Since then, I've been hooked on container gardening and have had so much fun growing a huge range of different plants, from stately-cut leaved Japanese maples to hanging baskets dripping with colour. Every year, I grow masses of plants in pots, old favourites as well as new varieties and every year, I get the most enormous pleasure from container gardening. I hope this book helps you enjoy it as much as I do!

Happy gardening!

Pots &Tubs

It's no wonder that gardening in pots and tubs is so popular. Virtually anything, from a majestic clipped bay tree to a simple clump of crocus, will happily thrive in pots. Simply by providing the right conditions, you can succeed with an incredible range of plants, including those that wouldn't like your garden soil but will flourish in a pot if you give it the right compost.

Watch out though, it can be pretty addictive. Once you've got the hang of it (and, honestly, it isn't difficult), your collection of pots will grow and grow. One lady I met has over 120 different pots of plants on her patio and, she told me with a huge smile, that there was still room for a few more!

Inspiring Ideas

Whether it's a simple plant in a pot or a colour themed extravaganza, there are many striking ways to use pots. Here are some ideas that inspired me.

Every pot doesn't have to be different. One of the simplest and most effective ways of creating extra impact is to plant several identical containers with the same plant (or planting scheme). Position them in a line, along the patio for instance, or up a flight of steps (**right**). This repeated planting will create a really striking yet harmonious effect.

Group other containers together in small clusters. Odd numbers always seem to look best (**below**). If you've a mix of different materials, such as terracotta, wood and plastic, separate them so that each has its own area.

Use your imagination and you'll find all sorts of things make effective containers. With inspiration they can even make impressive talking points (**above**).

When you're deciding on which container to use, pick one that is in proportion to its surroundings. A small pot looks out of place on its own on a huge patio whilst a big pot can overwhelm a small area. Also think about how it's going to blend in with the setting. Sleek looking plastic planters never look quite right in a traditional style cottage garden.

Choosing Containers

I use a variety of different pots in my garden. Each material has its own particular advantages and disadvantages.

Terracotta

For warm, natural beauty, nothing compares with terracotta pots. I just love them! There's a style to suit every patio and every budget, from the standard plain no nonsense flower pot to wonderfully ornate, handmade planters adorned with swags, garlands and cherubs (which remind me of certain QVC presenters). You can't go wrong with terracotta pots, they all look fabulous.

I like the way they mellow beautifully, looking even lovelier with age (a bit like us, then) and they're porous so water can seep through the sides, keeping plant roots cooler in hot summers while preventing waterlogging in winter. The downside is that they are rather brittle, so can break easily and can dry out quickly in warmer weather. I know to my cost that the less well made pots, especially the lighter pink versions, aren't frost proof and can shatter in a hard winter. So I always try to buy frost resistant pots or, even better, a frost proof pot (keep your receipt just in case).

Glazed Pots

These are sold in a variety of wonderful shapes and colours, and can brighten up any patio. Grasses, bamboos and maples look superb in the oriental style pots while yellow or white flowering plants look magical in blue glazed pots.

They're easy to clean (simply wipe them with a cloth) and they are often sold with saucers which can be helpful for summer watering. However, choose

Wood

Glazed

> **"When you're choosing a container, pick one that's in proportion to its surroundings. A small pot looks out of place on its own on a huge patio whilst a big pot can overwhelm a small area."**

with care as the bold colours and patterns don't suit every patio. Check them for drainage holes in the bottom before you buy. Some glazed pots don't have them (and they need them) and it's a real nuisance having to drill holes in them yourself.

Plastic

When I first started in gardening, you could only buy them in standard shapes in green, brown or white. Now, thank goodness, there's a wonderful selection in all shapes and colours, some even look uncannily like terracotta pots. As with most things in life, you get what you pay for. The cheapest pots may seem bargains but often don't last long. The more expensive pots are thicker, stronger and usually last years longer.

I use quite a few plastic pots as they are relatively inexpensive, as well as being lightweight and easy to move. They are also non-porous so they don't dry out as quickly as terracotta pots. The downside is that most plastic pots are relatively thin so they don't provide the plants with much protection from winter cold. In my experience, the cheaper pots do discolour and go brittle after a few years, especially if positioned in full sun. As for the colour of the pot, choose anything but black and white. White pots tend to get grubby with age while basic black pots not only look a bit ugly, they also absorb heat from the sun which can bake the plants' roots.

Stone effect

Terracotta

Wicker

Fibre/clay

Stone

For years, when I worked in a garden centre, the only stone pots that we sold were beautiful copies of the grand pots displayed in the gardens of stately homes. They were heavy, expensive and only suited very formal patios. Recently, I've been delighted to discover the reconstituted Terrazzo planters which are made from crushed stone (often marble or granite), which are mixed with cement and then cast in a wide range of shapes and sizes, in wonderful colours and often very contemporary styles.

 The other advantage over traditional stone is that reconstituted Terrazzo planters are relatively lightweight. When choosing, check for drainage holes at the bottom and bear in mind that the lighter planters can be very thin so they don't provide that much insulation for the plants' roots in winter

Wood

Another natural choice and there's something for every taste. Beautiful wood planters are sold in a great range of styles from eye-wateringly expensive contemporary style planters to rustic bark clad tubs. And for a huge, great value planter, you can't beat a traditional half barrel. One of the major benefits of wood is that it helps insulate plant roots from extremes of hot and cold. Also I like the fact that wooden planters can be

Top left: One of my much loved terracotta pots. Now over twenty years old, it has more than lived up to its frost proof guarantee.

Bottom left: Stone pots have a timeless elegance which suits more traditional gardens.

Right: Old chimney pots make a colourful focal point. It can take a lot of compost to fill them so the crafty alternative is to pop plastic pots inside the top and plant them up.

painted or stained in any colour you like. Hardwood containers cost more than those made in softwood but usually last longer. If you buy a softwood planter treat it once a year with a coat of paint or stain. That'll help prolong its life (and freshen it up too).

One disadvantage of wood is that moisture from the compost can cause it to slowly rot from the inside so, to minimise the problem, line the planter with a plastic sheet (with holes at the bottom for drainage). Or alternatively, simply pop in a plastic pot just smaller than the planter and plant that up. My one exception to the rule is that I don't line half barrels because the wood is best kept damp. If these barrels do dry out, the wood can shrink and the metal rings fall off (which, in my experience, means that the tub soon falls to bits).

Metal

Good for a modern, contemporary style garden, especially when planted with grasses, bamboos or shaped box. They're long-lasting, light and easy to clean but can heat up quickly in prolonged hot sun and bake the plants' roots. To help keep the heat out, line the inside (but not the bottom) with sheets of polystyrene or bubble-wrap polythene. Alternatively, fill with compost, make a planting hole in the top and pop in a plant growing in plastic pot. The compost will act as an insulator and protect the roots from overheating.

Wicker

Charming, natural looking, generally small planters. I think they look especially attractive filled with dwarf spring flowering bulbs. They're very cheap (especially if you recycle old houseplant baskets). However, they can decay quickly if not treated with polyurethane varnish (apply three coats ideally). For even longer life, line the inside with polythene to prevent damp soil from rotting the basket from the inside. Do make holes in the bottom of the polythene to allow water to drain out. Wicker baskets are best for spring and summer displays as they can look a little drab in winter.

Top: Metal containers create a very crisp, modern look but can over-heat in very sunny spots.

Bottom: Wicker adds natural style to the patio. A few coats of varnish will help preserve it.

Left: Wooden half barrels are good value and a great way to grow a wide range of plants in one container.

Below: An old pair of shoes
transformed into fun planters,
Simply bootiful!

Above: Burgon & Ball's prizewinning
garden at Hampton Court Flower
show featured flexible planters
disguised by wicker surrounds.

Unusual Containers

For a bit of fun, why not plant up something completely different? Almost anything can be used as a container as long as it can hold compost (you may need to line it with polythene) and has good drainage.

I once ran a Wacky container competition in a national newspaper and I was astonished by the variety of fun containers that the readers used. They included old footballs, decorative tea and biscuit tins, worn out trainers and wellies, a shop mannequin, a canoe and even a battered old tuba. It's eco-friendly recycling and it's huge fun. And it'll give you, as well as your friends and neighbours a bit of a laugh.

Flexible Planters

Over the past few years, partly in response to the interest in growing vegetables on the patio, a variety of flexible, reinforced plastic planters have been introduced. Simply fill with compost and pack them with plants.

The early versions, quite frankly, looked rather unattractive, a bit like grow bags on steroids, but now they're sold in much more natural styles, colours and patterns. Some are still too garish for my taste but are easily disguised with natural wicker surrounds (which you can buy separately although increasingly they're often sold as part of a kit with the planter).

Flexible planters are relatively good value and you can buy them in a range of shapes, sizes and depths to suit a wide range of crops from potatoes to tomatoes. The other advantage is that, once you've emptied them out at the end of the summer, they can be stored flat

Left: You can't make drainage holes in ceramic mugs like these so pop a generous layer of gravel in the bottom before planting up and any excess water will drain away into this.

over winter. Flexible planters often only last a couple of seasons or so, and I don't like the way that they bulge in the middle, making them look unsightly. This can be hidden by using those wicker surrounds or by simply placing a few pots in front of them.

Grow Bags

These are probably the cheapest 'containers' you can buy, essentially a decorative (!) bag of compost that you can pop on a sunny patio to grow crops (and flowers too). I love them, mind you one of my early jobs was as 'Assistant in charge of Gro-Bags' at one of our leading garden companies!

Watering is the biggest challenge with grow bags, especially with the smaller bags (that's one of the reasons I prefer the bigger versions which hold a generous 60 litre of compost). Grow bag waterers make the job much easier – simply pour water (or diluted plant feed) into the reservoir at one end and the water is quickly and evenly dispersed through a tube along the entire length of the bag.

Although they can be used to grow virtually anything from strawberries to French Beans, tomatoes are the most popular crop grown in grow bags (interestingly, they were originally developed for commercial tomato growers). For bigger and easier crops in grow bags, many gardeners use Grow Pots which sit in the centre of the bag, three pots (one per plant) per bag. Each circular pot has two compartments, you add water to the outer section and plant feed to the inner section (which is topped up with extra compost). It's claimed Grow Pots use up 30% less water but produce up to 40% more tomatoes.

At the end of the season, when the tomatoes have finished, take them out, add some controlled release fertiliser, and then plant the bag with lettuce or baby carrots, and get a second crop from it.

Growing Success

This is the important bit! Get the planting, watering and feeding right and your plants will thrive. Don't worry – it's not as difficult as you may think.

Choosing a Compost

Now, first things first. It may seem like a crafty, money–saving idea but please don't be tempted to use garden soil in your pots. It'll gradually compact down, squeezing the air out and your plants will really struggle. I've Yorkshire blood in me and I don't like spending money unless I have to. But potting compost is worth every penny. Most garden centres and DIY stores sell a bewildering range but essentially there are just two types.

Multi-purpose compost: I use this for bedding plants, vegetables and any plants that are going to be growing in their containers for just a few months. Multi-purpose compost holds water well (so it's especially useful for smaller containers that can dry out faster), it's lighter than soil based composts (important when the weight of the container could be an issue, such as on balconies), and it's clean and easy to handle.

Traditionally multi-purpose composts contain peat and these produce consistently good results and have continued to be my preferred choice. However, for environmental reasons, gardeners are being encouraged to use non peat-based composts based on green waste or wood fibre. The quality and consistency of these used to be very variable but they've improved and I'm happier with them than I once was. After running many trials with various multi-purpose composts, everything from all peat to no peat, I've been most impressed with a special reduced peat mix, containing around 70% peat and 30% wood fibre. This is the compost that I prefer to use.

John Innes compost: I use this compost for shrubs, climbers, trees, roses, fruit, herbs, hardy perennials such as hostas and anything that is going to be growing in its container for more than a year. John Innes composts contain loam as well as peat and sand, so they retain water well but, importantly, don't tend to get waterlogged (this is particularly important in winter). They're also heavier so add a bit of weight and stability. There's a range to choose from. I use John Innes No. 2 for virtually all my perennial plants but if I'm planting an older tree, shrub or climbing rose, then I would pick the slightly more nutrient rich John Innes No. 3.

For lime hating plants, such as azaleas, rhododendrons, camellias, pieris and blueberries, use John Innes Ericaceous compost.

Compost Additives

I know you're itching to get planting, but just before you do, there are a few products which can be added to the compost at planting time that can help you save time and effort during the summer.

One of the secrets of success for fantastic containers, baskets and window boxes is to feed your plants regularly. I'm a great believer in regular feeding with a plant food (especially Flower Power, of course!) and, in my experience, that produces the very best results. However, if regular feeding isn't possible, or you just can't be bothered, then it's well worth adding some controlled release fertiliser granules to the compost when planting up.

Above: This attractive stand is a striking way to display individual pots of flowers. The bright blue colour really helps it stand out.

Left: A good multi-purpose compost suits annual plants but longer lived plants, like most of these, prefer a John Innes compost.

These cleverly release minute amounts of fertiliser throughout the growing season and that's enough to keep less vigorous plants growing quite happily. The downside is that, for fast growing summer bedding plants and flowers as well as top cropping fruits and vegetables, they don't provide enough nutrients to get the best out of the plants so, if possible, I'd suggest an occasional supplementary feed with an extra high potash feed such as Flower Power.

Moisture retention crystals are a great boon for low maintenance gardeners. When mixed with water, the sugar like crystals expand into a gel which acts like a mini water reservoir and, when added to the compost, can halve the number of times you have to water your plants in summer. They're a brilliant time saver for summer containers but I prefer not to use them in winter planters as the compost can become waterlogged.

For ease of use, you can buy special combination products which contain water crystals and controlled release fertiliser. The quality of these does vary, make sure you buy packs containing controlled release feed, rather than the less effective, but cheaper, slow release feed.

Container Magic does even more as it helps in three ways. It is a special blend of naturally occurring, water-retaining crystals in two sizes, small granules for instant water retention and rapid release as well as larger granules for slower release (so it is more effective in drier weather). In addition, it includes a special Flower Power controlled release boost feed to help establish plants in the first crucial weeks after planting.

The third ingredient is naturally occurring mycorrhizal fungi which attach themselves to the plants' roots, helping them absorb more nutrients and water so that the plants grow better and are more drought tolerant. Five weeks after planting, the boost feed has done its job, and you should start regular feeding with your normal plant food.

In my trials (see photos right), my Container Magic treated begonias grew almost double the size of non-treated plants when measured at the end of the season. Interestingly, the size difference became most noticeable from August onwards when the root systems had grown big enough to really benefit from the mycorrhizal fungi.

Above: Both begonia plants were treated equally in my trials but the one at the bottom had Container Magic added to the compost at planting time.

Left: An old wooden barrow filled with pots of primulas creates a really attractive feature in this garden.

Planting Up

Once you've chosen your potting compost and any compost additives it's time to get creative. This is the fun bit!

Sort Out the Drainage

If you're new to gardening, you'll probably think this sounds a bit boring and you might be tempted to skip it. Please don't, it's really important. All plants (well, ok, there are a few exceptions like water lilies) need decent drainage when growing in containers to make sure that any excess water can drain away. Otherwise the compost can get soggy and the plants' roots rot, killing the plants.

So good drainage is essential! First of all, check your container has holes in the bottom. If not, you'll have to make some. Next, you need to prevent the compost from blocking up the drainage holes by placing a layer of drainage material at the bottom of the pot (**1**). You can use crocks (the gardener's name for broken bits of terracotta pots), polystyrene chips, large pebbles or stones. Some terracotta pots have just a single drainage hole, cover this first, and then add the extra drainage material. As a rule of thumb, small pots need 13mm/0.5in of drainage, up to 5cm/2in of drainage in larger containers and up to 15cm/6in in a half barrel (I use broken tiles for these).

Get Planting

Firstly, water your plants. Dry plants never seem to establish as quickly in containers even if you give them loads of water after planting up. Then fill up the container with compost to the point where the base of the plant will sit. If the compost is lumpy, break it down with your hands. Next, mix in any compost additives such as Container Magic (**2**).

Place the plant(s) in position and fill in with more compost (plus a sprinkling more of any additives you are using), taking care not to leave any air pockets, and firm them in (**3**). Gently level off the compost at 2.5–5cm/1–2in below the rim depending on the size of the pot, to allow room for watering. Then water the plants in. If I'm planting in spring or summer, I water them in with a plant feed to really give them a kick start.

You might find that this first watering makes the compost settle down slightly lower than you want. If so, simply top up or fill in any gaps with extra compost.

Finishing Touches

As a finishing touch, you can add a layer of mulch (**4**). These are usually decorative materials, like glass pebbles, slate or gravel, which are placed on top of the compost. Mulches reduce evaporation so the compost doesn't dry out as quickly (meaning less watering), enhances the look of your planting, prevents the weeds from growing and can deter slugs and snails. The downside I find is that it's a bit more difficult to tell when the plants need watering as you can't see when the compost is dry. If in doubt you have to put your finger through the mulch to check. By the way, when using mulches, don't overfill. You still need a minimum of 2.5cm/1in space from the top of the mulch to the top of the container to allow for watering.

That's the creative part done, and hopefully, you're pretty pleased with how it looks. How well it grows from now on is up to you! It's basically all down to keeping on top of the watering and feeding.

Planting a Climber

For best results with climbers in pots, pick a container at least 45cm/18in wide and ideally just as deep. If possible I always like to grow a few plants around the base of the climber to create an even prettier display. Spring and summer bedding plants or evergreen perennials look especially good. Half fill your container with John Innes compost No. 3 and plant the climber in the centre (**1**). Clematis prefer to be planted slightly deeper than other climbers, ideally 5cm/2in of their stem should buried beneath the surface of the compost. Then add a climbing frame or make a wigwam from sturdy bamboo canes (**2**). Plant around the sides of the container then detach the climber from the small canes it was grown on and wind the plant around the climbing frame in a spiral and tie it in.

Left: This clematis has been grown on a framework of canes and some metal spirals have been added afterwards for extra decoration.

2

Topiary in Pots

Traditional Topiary, in the shape of spirals, pyramids or domes, adds an air of year-round elegance to any garden. You can buy ready shaped topiary, usually box (buxus), from garden centres and DIY stores and pot them up for the patio. For a bit of fun, you can also buy topiary frames in a variety of shapes, pop them over a young box plant in a pot and grow your own!

Watering

Keeping your plants looking their best requires regular attention to prevent them drying out. But thankfully there are ways to make your life easier.

Plants in containers need watering all year round except in freezing conditions. In the summer, on a hot, sunny patio, you may need to water your container every day but in the winter, it might be as little as every two to three weeks. Experienced gardeners will tell you to simply water your plants whenever they need it – which is a fat lot of help if you've only just started gardening!

Over time, you will be able to judge when plants need watering, often by simply looking at the colour of the compost (which works for John Innes and Multi-purpose compost, but not for coir compost, which is one reason I don't use it). For less experienced gardeners, just put your finger in the top couple of centimetres of compost. If it feels dry it's time to water.

Making Watering Even Easier

Wetting agents such as Wet n Gro are a real boon. This special detergent like liquid helps the compost retain water better so you don't have to water as often and, as an added benefit, you use less water too. Simply add 5ml to 4.5l/1 gallon of water and water it on. It works its magic for around one month, but, over time, gradually washes out, so you need to repeat the treatment every four weeks in the summer.

Water retention crystals or Container Magic can halve the number of times you have to water your container in the summer. Simply mix them in with the compost when planting up.

Watering spikes even do the watering for you! Some years ago, Garden Innovations introduced the remarkable bottle top watering spikes. Fitted to a recycled soft drinks bottle, filled with water or diluted plant food, they can water a container for up to three weeks. The really clever part is the dripper which automatically adjusts the amount of water released according to the temperature. So the warmer it is, and the more your

Top: I enjoy watering my containers in the summer but it can take ages so I'm all for making it as easy as possible!

Bottom: Water spikes can be attached to water flasks, like this, or old drinks bottles and they will automatically water plants as they need it.

plants need water, the faster it waters them! The water is delivered directly to the roots of the plants, so less water is lost through evaporation.

Recycled drinks bottles are, to be fair, a bit of an eyesore so I generally recommend using them only for holiday watering (when you can't see them). If you want to use the spikes for day to day watering, fit them onto green watering flasks which are also sold by Garden Innovations. These flasks are far more attractive than old drinks bottles and they're compact enough to be hidden behind the plants in bigger containers.

Automated Watering Systems

For the easiest of all options, it's worth thinking about an automated system. They're understandably very popular in hotter countries like Australia but they've taken a while to catch on here, partly because they were a bit fiddly to set up. But now they've become easier and cheaper too. At its simplest, it's a drip watering system whereby a series of adjustable heads, positioned in containers and baskets, are connected by plastic tubing to a hose. Turn on the tap and all the containers are watered at once.

The minor drawback is that it can take a little while to set up the system so to save the hassle, Hozelock introduced Aquapods (an idea suggested by one of my gardening heroes, Peter Seabrook) and this only takes about 5 minutes to set up. Each pod contains five drippers, which can be used independently of each other. Pull them out of the pod, clip them in the containers, connect the pod to the tap and that's it. And if you've more than five containers, you can easily add enough extra units to water up to 39 pots at a time. At the end of the summer, it takes just a few seconds to pack each pod away for the coming year.

For the ultimate in easy watering, connect your Aquapod, or indeed any watering system, to a special

The Aquapod automatic watering system in operation. The black tubes needn't be this obvious, they are best hidden behind the plants!

timer. You set the time when watering starts and ends, and how much water is needed. It's a great timesaver if you're away a lot or on holiday, or if you simply just can't be bothered with watering.

The slight disadvantage to any of these automatic systems is that the black tubing can be difficult to hide and it can look a bit unsightly. Also you still need to feed your plants. Mind you, professional growers use automatic watering systems with built in feeders so with any luck it won't be long until these are adapted for home gardeners.

Watering Know-how

❀ If possible, during the summer, water in the early evening or morning to give it time to soak in and reach the roots before the day warms up and the water begins to evaporate.

❀ It's difficult to give a guide as to how much water to give your containers as it will depend on the position (they dry out faster in bright sun or wind compared with a sheltered shady spot), the type of container (terracotta pots are porous so water evaporates through their sides, hence they need more watering than plastic pots which aren't porous), and the type of plant (fast growing large plants generally need more water than slow growing small plants). **As a rule of thumb, a big pot, say around 45cm/18in diameter, can need up to 4.5 litres/1 gallon per day in sunny, dry weather.** A smaller pot, 20cm/10in, of summer bedding plants would probably need half this amount.

❀ **Give the plants a good soaking so that all the compost gets wet. If you only give them a light sprinkling, then only the top layer gets the moisture and, over time, your plants won't grow as well as they could.**

❀ **If in doubt, when you're watering, give them a bit more. Any excess water should drain away.**

"Keep these tips in mind and you won't go far wrong!"

🌼 In hot weather, pop your smaller pots on saucers. They'll hold any water that has drained out of the pot and this will be absorbed back into the compost as it dries out.

🌼 **Don't assume, just because it's been raining, that your plants have had plenty of water. Often the leaves act like an umbrella so most of the rain bounces off and never reaches the compost.**

🌼 Don't panic if the pots get a bit dry from time to time. It happens to us all and the plants will soon perk up once they're watered. It's more of a problem when the compost really dries out. Usually, John Innes composts are easy to re-wet, especially if you add a few drops of washing up liquid or Wet n Gro to the watering can. Multi-purpose composts can be more challenging especially when the compost shrinks away from the sides. When this happens, and you water, it pours over the surface of the bone dry compost and down the gaps between the pot and the compost! It's a blooming nuisance but there is a nifty way to sort it out. Submerse the pot in a bowl of water that is deep enough to allow the water to cover the top of the compost. Leave it there until the bubbles stop, usually a few minutes, then remove the container from the water and leave in the shade for a few hours until the plants recover.

🌼 **It's impractical to submerge really large pots, so try re-wetting them using a watering can fitted with a watering rose or a hose fitted with a hose-end sprayer. The gentle water pattern penetrates the compost much more easily than a solid stream of water.**

Feeding Your Plants

I'm passionate about this! It's probably one of the most important things you need to know about container gardening.

Regular feeding can transform an ordinary planted container into a spectacular showstopper! Dr Arnie Rainbow, one of our leading and most respected garden scientists, has run plant trials for many years and told me, in an interview, that he is 'often asked how some people have greenfingers and largely it's down to good feeding of your plants'.

Most composts contain basic nutrients which are claimed to feed your plants for the first few weeks and for autumn and winter planted containers, they do. However, in my experience, it pays to start feeding most spring and summer planted containers straight away. There's a huge range of plant feeds sold at garden centres and DIY stores. Here are the key things you need to know before you buy.

General Purpose Feeds

These are formulated to feed everything from rubber plants to cabbages and they'll keep your plants ticking over very nicely. But for more flowers, fruits and vegetables, you should use an extra high potash feed like Flower Power.

These nutrient packed feeds can make an amazing difference to your plants. In an independent trial, tomato plants fed with the brand leading general purpose fertiliser produced an average crop of 2.5kg of tomatoes per plant. Identical plants, grown under identical conditions, but fed with Flower Power

All plants including spring flowering bulbs will benefit from regular feeding.

produced an average of 6.3kg of tomatoes per plant – that's over double the crop. If you can achieve this with tomatoes, imagine what your geraniums, begonias, fuchsias, strawberries – indeed any flowering or fruiting plants – could look like. To get an idea, take a look at some of the plants grown by home gardeners using Flower Power, they're on the customer review section on my website, www.richardjacksonsgarden.co.uk. I hope the pictures and comments (a number of which are from first-time gardeners) will convince you of the huge benefits of using extra high potash plant food.

Soluble powder feeds need to be dissolved in water. Simply add a scoop of the feed to 4.5 litres/ 1 gallon of water, stir well and water around the roots of the plants. Some soluble feeds, like Flower Power, can also be applied through special hose-end feeders.

Liquid feeds are easy to use but tend to cost more per gallon of diluted feed than soluble powder/ crystal feeds. Pour the concentrated liquid into the measure, add to the watering can, fill with water, stir and water the plants. For the ultimate in convenience, you can also buy ready to use liquid fertilisers that have already been diluted. Just pour and feed. This is an incredibly expensive way of feeding plants – a triumph of marketing over common sense. Save your money and buy some extra plants instead!

Controlled release fertilizers are added to the compost at planting time and feed your plants with low levels of general purpose fertiliser most of the summer. They save the hassle of remembering to feed but, in my experience, when growing summer bedding, fruit and vegetables, you'll get much better results using a soluble or liquid feed. If you use controlled release fertiliser in summer containers, you should give

Feeding strawberries and other fruit with a high potash fertiliser will help them produce bigger and tastier crops.

your plants some supplementary feeding from time to time. This is especially important from the end of July onwards as by then many controlled release fertilisers have virtually run out of nutrients.

Fertiliser sticks and tablets are controlled release fertiliser granules stuck together in clusters which can be pushed into the compost after planting. I'm a bit wary of them as if they are pushed in too close to the roots, the concentrated feed can cause scorch.

Feeding Know-how

❀ **When to feed** Feed your plants in the growing season from March until September. If using Flower Power, I'd recommend feeding **once a week in April and May**, then **twice a week from June until September**. This is especially important if you're growing summer flowering bedding plants or crops in pots, all of which really do that much better if well fed.

❀ **How much should you feed?** **It's a tricky one to answer as it depends on how many plants in the pot, their size, and how quickly they are growing. As a rule of thumb, I'd give 1–2 litres of diluted feed to a 20cm/8in pot and 4.5 litres/1 gallon to a 45cm/18in tub.**

Long-term Care

After you've invested all that time and money you'll want to keep pots looking their best for as long as possible. Here's how.

Deadheading

To keep flowering plants blooming as long as possible, cut off any fading or dead flowers. I generally check my plants every few days and use secateurs, flower snips or scissors to do the job. Softer shoots, on summer bedding plants, can be pinched out between finger and thumb. Deadheading helps in two ways. It stops the plant wasting energy on producing seeds and uses that energy to produce more flowers instead. It also tidies up the plant so it looks neater.

Moving Containers

It can be back breaking work moving heavy pots around the patio. If you need to do it regularly, for instance when you're cleaning the patio, then it's worth considering buying a pot mover. They're like posh sack trollies which let you move a pot weighing up to 50kg with remarkable ease.

Alternatively you could put the pots on plant movers, which are basically big saucers on wheels, so you can simply push the pot to one side when needed. If you're planning to keep the pot on the saucer all the time (which most people do) make sure you drill some holes in it for drainage.

Above: Annual top-dressing will help rejuvenate plants that have been growing in a container for more than one year. Remove the top layer of compost and fibrous fibrous roots (**top**). Replace this with fresh John Innes compost (**middle**) and sprinkle in some controlled release fertiliser (**bottom**). Firm down and water well.

Re-potting

After a year or so, depending on the size of container that you're using, perennial plants, like roses, trees and shrubs, may out-grow their pot. The tell-tale signs are a mass of congested roots in the pot, often followed by a lack of vigour. Simply re-pot the plants into a container one size larger (around 5cm/2in bigger). If the roots are really congested, gently tease them apart by hand or with a hand fork, and shake out some of the old, spent compost, before re-potting.

Top Dressing

If, however, your plants are already growing in as big a pot as you want (or can handle), then give the plants a new lease of life by using a professional technique called top dressing. Every spring, scrape away the top 7.5cm/3in of compost and replace it with fresh compost. When I top dress 'non-flowering' plants, like box bushes or bay trees, I also add some controlled release fertiliser to the layer of fresh compost to give them a gentle boost through the summer. I don't bother to add controlled release feed when topdressing flowering plants as they do much better with regular feeds of Flower Power.

Winter Care

For a period of years, we experienced a series of mild winters and that lulled some of us, including me, who live in the South of the country, into a false sense of security. A couple of years ago, we then had a very

Left: This beautiful Japanese maple will benefit from annual top dressing. The plants at the base will need to be temporarily dug out beforehand then replanted afterwards.

Right: Bubble-wrap isn't pretty but it does a great job in protecting pots and plants through harsh winters.

cold winter and it killed my beautiful potted bay trees positioned in pride of place either side of the front door. I was heartbroken – so my advice is to learn from my mistake and protect any slightly tender plants over winter just in case it turns very cold.

Wrap the plants in layers of horticultural fleece (available from most garden centres and DIY stores) before the winter turns freezing cold. If possible, also move the pot to a sheltered spot, away from biting cold winds. Take the fleece off when the weather warms up in the spring.

If a big freeze is forecast, it's also worth taking an extra precaution of insulating the pot as well. Wrap the sides in bubble-wrap to reduce the risk of the root-ball freezing. If it freezes for too long, the plants aren't able to draw any water from the roots and can, in extreme circumstances, die (usually in the spring, just as they start growing again). Evergreen plants are the most vulnerable but even deciduous plants (those that lose their leaves in winter) can be affected.

Hanging Baskets & Planters

I love hanging baskets! They have the most extraordinary impact. Just one basket flowering happily all summer can completely transform the dullest of areas.

Use them wherever you can, by the front doors, on the balcony, along the side of the house or to brighten up a dull fence. In the summer, cram them full of bedding plants or grow an edible feast of strawberries, tomatoes or herbs. In the winter, give them a new lease of life with winter flowering violas, colourful evergreens and spring bulbs.

Hanging baskets aren't as easy to look after as pots, especially in the summer. But nothing else will give you as much impact in such a small space. These are the real showstoppers for your garden.

Inspiring Ideas

Whether it's a flower filled ball of colour or an eye-catching edible feast, there are so many different ways to plant and enjoy your hanging baskets. I especially liked these ideas.

Double the impact with two hanging baskets and create something as impressive as the ones in the photo (**below**). For best effect, plant them up as matching baskets and hang either side of a door or at the same height on a wall or fence. Watch out though, when baskets grow this big it can be a struggle to get in the front door!

When baskets are as attractive as this (**above**) you don't want to cover them with trailing plants. Make a feature of them and simply plant some colourful bedding plants in the top.

Colourful foliage plants can create just as much impact as flowering plants. Here (**left**) golden creeping jenny (lysimachia) trails from the base of the basket adding an extra element of beauty and interest. Variegated ivy, silver leaved lamium, dark leaved ajuga and silver helichrysum are just as effective and they can provide longer lasting colour than many flowering plants. Last summer, I also experimented with exotic leaved coleus and was really pleased with the results.

Baskets and Liners

A fair few years ago when I started gardening you could only buy traditional wire baskets. Now there's much more choice and variety.

Wire Baskets

The traditional choice and generally the cheapest. For a really full, lush effect, you should plant the sides of wire baskets as well as the top. Smaller baskets (around 25cm/10in diameter) hold less compost, dry out faster and need more watering while the biggest baskets (40cm/16in) create the best displays but can be very heavy once planted (weighing as much as a hefty 25kg when watered). If I have the choice, I prefer 35cm/14in baskets which, surprisingly, hold 50% more compost than a 30cm/12in basket, have plenty of room for plants and aren't too heavy.

Wire baskets are relatively long lasting, you should get at least five years use from them. I also like the open mesh design which allows you to place plants where you like when planting the sides. However, wire baskets need lining with moss, coir or a readymade liner. They also take a fair amount of time to plant properly. I reckon I spend around 45 minutes per basket if I'm completely planting the sides and top. It's the sides that take the most time.

In my experience, the chains are the most vulnerable part so do check them once a year and buy replacements if needed. I was really upset once when my newly (and beautifully!) planted basket plummeted to the ground when the chains broke. It's also worth bearing in mind that it's difficult to use bigger plants when planting the sides. Generally, only smaller plants can be coaxed through the sides in the mesh. They can look a little unkempt to begin with but, believe me, they will soon fill out.

> **"Wire baskets are relatively long lasting, you should get at least five years use from them. I also like the open mesh design which allows you to place plants where you want."**

Easyfill Baskets

These are ingenious. A sturdy plastic basket with removable panels that enable you to plant the sides of the basket quickly and easily. Simply remove a panel, place the plant in the gap, pop the panel back in position and this will hold the plant securely in position.

Easyfill baskets have, deservedly, become very popular because planting the sides of the basket is much easier and the side planting panels enable you to use larger, flowering size plants so the basket looks more established. You don't need a liner with them either and there's a small water reservoir at the base which means they need slightly less watering.

Solid Baskets

Solid sided baskets are the easiest and quickest to plant. They're available in polythene lined wicker and plastic versions, and my choice would be the wicker as they look far more attractive All you have to do is pop a few plants in the top. They don't need a liner and they dry out less quickly. But you can't create quite as colourful a display with these as you can with a side planted basket. For the best effect, plant upright plants in the centre and trailing plants around the edge, they'll cascade down the sides and create a very pretty effect.

Babylon Bowls

Cleverly developed by engineer, Richard Conway, to overcome the limitations of hanging baskets, these are easy to plant and you can create impressive bowls of colour in a matter of minutes. The bowl is created by a circle of wide curved prongs made of nylon coated steel and it sits on a special wall mounted bracket so there are no chains to restrict the growth of the plants or swing in the wind. The plants are held in place by hefty wedges of moss which act as a water and nutrient reservoir.

I like them because they are so easy to plant, the job's done in minutes. You can use bigger, flowering size plants, the bowl can look good immediately. They last for years, much longer than most hanging baskets and the bowl can be rotated so all the plants can grow evenly (in most hanging baskets, plants at the back sometimes get less light and don't grow as well).

Top: Solid sided baskets look much more attractive when the plastic is disguised by colourful trailing plants.

Bottom: Wicker baskets have a charming natural style that suits any style of garden.

Wall Planters

They're the easy and almost instant way to transform boring walls and fences by covering them with columns of colour. For some years, gardeners have achieved the effect using cheap and cheerful flower pouches (which are like mini-grow bags which hang on a wall) but they need careful watering to look their best. Recently a new generation of more sophisticated wall planters has been introduced. These have built in watering tubes, so are much easier to care for and they produce spectacular displays.

Flower pouches: These are the original, simple, flexible, re-inforced plastic sleeves that are filled with compost, planted (using the pre-cut holes) and hung up on nail, screw or bracket. They're inexpensive (keep an eye out as they're quite often given away free in promotions) but watering can be a challenge. The pouches need to be thoroughly watered so that the plants in the bottom get as much water as those in the top. The trick is to check by squeezing the bottom corners, water should gently trickle out.

Polanters: Colourful, interlocking rigid plastic tubes that have a built in seep hose to make watering easier. Simply connect the hosepipe to the connector on the polanter, switch on at low pressure and the entire tube is evenly watered. The sturdy and long lasting planter is provided with brackets so that it's easy to fix to walls and fences. When planting up, add controlled release fertiliser granules to the compost as it's the easiest way to feed them. If you can't use a hosepipe for watering, the makers are bringing out a watering spike that enables you to water (and feed) using old drinks bottles.

Flower towers: A good value planter for walls as well as patios. It's made of recycled material, stands up to 90cm/3ft tall and holds up to 30 plug plant sized plants. The really clever part is the special watering tube which ensures even watering throughout the planter (so you get even growth). Simply pour water (or diluted plant food) into the top and that's it! They reckon it only takes 10 seconds to do the watering.

Top: Wall baskets can transform the look of an ugly fence or wall.

Bottom: Flower pouches on trial at Thompson & Morgan. For low cost planters, they're difficult to beat.

Left: A pretty cottage made even prettier by the colourful hanging baskets and planters.

Top: Probably the most stylish wall basket I've seen. Beautifully planted too.

Bottom: Normally I'd suggest disguising the liner with plants but this basket is so ornate that it deserves to be seen.

Right: Once the plants establish, the liner is completely hidden and its only job is to stop the compost from falling out!

Liners

The open mesh design of many baskets may be perfect for planting but it does have the rather major drawback that it doesn't hold the compost in! So we use liners to stop the compost from falling through the gaps. Some liners enhance the look of the basket while others certainly don't! So choose with care.

Moss: If I'm lining a wire basket this is my first choice. It's easy to use and looks (and is!) natural. By far the best way to buy it is in its compressed form (sold under various names including Big Moss). One slab of Big Moss (which looks like a big flat Weetabix) produces enough moss to line up to eight 30cm/12in baskets. Simply cut or break off a section, pop it in a bucket of water and leave it there for a few minutes to expand. This type of moss is better quality, holds more water and is much better value than the packs of spongy moss normally sold in garden centres. One tip when lining the basket, pat it between your hands and make it into sheets about 3cm/1.25in thick.

Coir: Another natural product, often pre-formed to fit the basket. I'm not a great fan of this as you have to cut planting holes in the side, which can be a struggle, and it doesn't hold water as well as moss. I recently looked after a friend's baskets which were lined with coir and It's was a nightmare keeping them well watered in warm weather. Not worth buying! Also birds sometime peck them to pieces as the coir is great for their nests!

Wood fibre preformed liners: Avoid at all costs. They're ugly, inflexible, don't hold water and it's rather difficult to make holes in them if you want to plant the sides.

Wool: This natural liner insulates the plants' roots, holds water better than coir but is difficult to cut and can look quite ugly until the plants grow enough to disguise it.

Recycled fibre liners: As an alternative to moss, these are easy to use as they come with pre-cut planting holes, look reasonably natural (from a distance), hold water better than coir and are lined with polythene to help with water retention.

Growing Success

For a breathtaking basket, you need to pamper your plants. Here's how.

Compost

I won't be popular with the manufacturers for saying it but my advice is to ignore all the pricey, specialist container and hanging basket composts. John Innes composts are a bit too heavy for baskets and put extra strain on your back (when hanging up the basket) as well as the bracket so my tip is to use good multi-purpose compost.

Moisture Retaining Crystals

These are invaluable for summer baskets which can dry out extremely quickly in the warmer months. They can halve the number of times you need to water during the summer months. I use Container Magic for best results and this is added to the compost at planting time.

Picking the Plants

I always love this part! For wire baskets, you need choose some young plants to pop through the sides of the baskets but the top can take larger plants if you prefer. Jumbo plug plants, often sold in mid-late spring, are the perfect size for popping through the gaps in the sides. Easyfill baskets and Babylon bowls are best planted with larger, flowering size plants – they're more expensive to buy but the planters generally look pretty and colourful straight away.

Hopefully you've grown on some of the plants yourself. Do try, it's really easy. Simply buy some plug plants in early spring, pot them on and they'll romp away on a windowsill until planting up time. By then, they should be as good as those in the garden centre and, if you've grown a fair few, have saved you a small fortune.

If you're buying the plants for your basket, choose the sturdiest, bushiest available. Don't pick those with any sign of disease or yellowing, any which are spindly or are very light (they've got too dry).

Left: To get results as good as this, it's simply down to watering, feeding and deadheading.

Right: It's best to be generous with your planting if you want to create a mouth-watering display of colour.

Planting Up

When to Plant

If you're planning a basket for summer colour, the usual time for planting up is from May to early June. Most summer flowering bedding plants aren't frost hardy so if you put the basket out before the last frosts have finished, you may need to protect them some nights by covering with a plant fleece. If you don't want to take the risk, wait until the last frosts have passed.

As a rule, it's early May for protected coastal areas and bigger towns in the South. Wait until mid May for most central areas and late May/early June for the North and colder spots, but do watch the weather forecasts in case there's an unexpected late frost.

If you're lucky enough to have somewhere like a heated greenhouse to give your basket some frost protection, you can plant it early, the plants will grow quickly and by the time you put it outside for the summer, the plants will have established and have instant impact. Don't put it out straight away, acclimatise the plants to the colder conditions by putting the basket outside in the day and bringing it at night for a fortnight (it's called hardening off).

For autumn/winter/spring baskets, I think the ideal time planting up time is September. Your plants then have a few weeks to settle in and establish themselves before the colder weather sets in.

Planting a Wire Basket

Set the basket on a bowl or bucket to keep it steady and line the base with moss, firming it down so that there's a good thick layer that won't leak compost (**1**). You might like to place a plastic saucer or piece of polythene over this, to help retain water. Top up with compost (mixing in Container Magic if required) to the level of the moss.

Set your first circle of plants close to the base, about 7.5cm/3in apart. Working from the inside of the basket, wrap the leaves in a tube of newspaper and carefully work this through pass this through the gap in the wire mesh, being as gentle as possible with the roots, so that the rootball is resting on the compost (**2**).

Top up with more moss and compost and add a second circle of plants, positioned so that they don't directly overhang those below them (**3**). Carry on this way until you reach the top of the basket. Larger baskets will happily accommodate three circles of plants, and they'll produce an amazing looking, lush effect.

Finally, plant up the top of the basket (**4**). In a mixed basket, use the main plant as the centre-piece, an upright geranium for instance, and fill around it with smaller growing bush plants and a few trailers. Fill in any gaps with more compost and top up any sunken areas which

"**Whatever type of basket you're planting up, always water the plants well beforehand. This helps to keep the rootball intact as moist compost allows you to tease the plants apart, rather than tear them.**"

appear once you've given the basket a good soaking. I always use diluted plant food for this first watering.

Baskets with wool or fibre mat liners are planted in much the same way as moss lined baskets. The only challenge is if you need to make additional planting holes around the sides. Wool is reasonably pliable and can be pulled apart or cut in situ, but with fibre liners it's easiest to make the holes beforehand.

Planting Other Baskets

Easyfill baskets are wonderfully simple to plant and, if you're using bigger plants, give an almost instant effect.

Planting up plastic pot baskets is just like planting a pot. All you have to do is plant the top! But try to plant a few trailing plants around the edge to cascade over and disguise the sides.

Polanters and Flower Towers are equally easy, just fill them up with compost layer by layer, planting as you go. The only secret is that you should firmly push the compost in, so you don't leave any air pockets.

Planting Babylon bowls is a bit like building a wall. Set in the liner (supplied with the bowl), add a thin layer of compost, then place the first layer of plants in between the curved 'fingers' of the bowl. Fill in the gaps between the rootballs with wads of tightly rolled moss (I like Big Moss), then add a second layer of plants, placing them above the lower layer of moss and then pack these in position with more moss. Fill the centre of the basket with more compost and then plant the top.

Far left: An Easyfill basket a few weeks after planting.

Top: The Easyfill basket can be quickly planted up using bigger, more established plants.

Bottom: The planting holes in the Polanter are the ideal size for plug plants like these trailing geraniums.

Watering

The beauty of hanging baskets is that they hold so many plants you can get an amazingly colourful display. But to achieve it, you have to keep them well watered. So check them regularly. The hotter, or windier the position, the faster they can dry out.

✿ Most gardeners use watering cans but they are rather heavy when full and it can be difficult to lift the can high enough to reach the basket. I know a fair few gardeners who use 1 litre/2 pint plastic bottles for watering, they're far less heavy than cans.

✿ Alternatively, instead of lifting a watering can up to the basket, bring the basket down to waist height, by using the ingenious Hi-Lo pulley – as you can see in the photo on the left. Fitted onto the hanging basket bracket, it simply allows you to lower the basket for watering (as well as general tidying up and deadheading). They're ideal for smaller baskets, larger baskets can be too heavy for them to operate smoothly. Models vary so check the maximum weight recommendations before you buy.

❀ If you prefer watering with a hosepipe, keep the water pressure low or you might blast some of the compost out and make a right mess. Hanging basket lances are great, you can reach the basket easily and the gentle spray doesn't damage the flowers.

❀ **A slightly cheaper option is to use a hose-end feeder – see left. These have the additional (and obvious!) advantage as they can be used to feed your plants whilst gently watering them.**

❀ For summer baskets, the best time to water is in the evening or early morning when less water will be lost through evaporation. I find a wetting agent, such as Wet n Gro, added to the water once a month, makes watering much easier as it helps the compost absorb and hold water more effectively.

❀ **If the worst happens and the basket dries out completely, it will probably be tricky to re-wet it so take it down completely and soak it in a bowl of water for an hour or so until the compost is thoroughly soaked.**

Feeding and Aftercare

If you've ever wondered why some people have the knack of growing beautiful baskets and others don't, the difference is usually due to how they've fed them and kept them tidy.

Feeding

Hanging baskets are amongst the most intensive growing conditions possible – a small volume of compost is supporting a large number of vigorously growing plants. Regular feeding is essential if all of them are going to flourish. Feed your baskets twice a week in the summer with extra high potash feed like Flower Power. It will make a huge difference.

After banging on about the importance of feeding, you might feel slightly surprised when I suggest that you don't feed your winter baskets every week. It can actually do more harm than good during the colder months (as the plants aren't growing much, if at all). Wait until the early spring, when the weather warms up and then start feeding them regularly.

Deadheading

It's a bit of a chore picking off the finished flowers, but it really pays off. Not only will it keep the baskets looking tidy, it stops the plants from going to seed and that means even more flowers.

Trimming

Inevitably, some of the trailing plants get a bit straggly during the summer. Pinch or cut them back every few weeks to encourage them to bush out, look tidier and not swamp the rest of the plants.

Top: Pinching out finished flowers stops them from going to seed.

Bottom: For longer stemmed flowers, it's easier to deadhead them by cutting with scissors, snips or secateurs.

Left: I try to deadhead my baskets every two to three days in the summer.

Window Boxes

Window boxes are marvellous – mini-gardens
neatly packed in small spaces that will really
brighten up a windowsill or balcony. Cram
them with summer bedding or fill them with
a feast of aromatic herbs or flavour filled
vegetables. Then re-plant in the autumn to
bring some much needed colour to the drab
winter months.

The great thing about window boxes is that,
generally, they need a lot less pampering than
hanging baskets. So, in effect, you can get
maximum results with minimum effort!

Inspiring Ideas

Well planted window boxes are a real joy.
Plants look so good 'framed' by the window.
Here's some planting ideas that I like.

If you're lucky enough to have the space for the plants to really cascade, make a real splash by planting the front of your window box with vigorous trailing plants to create a real waterfall of colour (**right**). The most vigorous plants in this box are the surfinia petunias which could be omitted from your planting scheme if you wanted a slightly more compact look.

Many people don't bother with autumn window boxes but they're missing a treat. I really like this simple but very effective look of red berried skimmia edged either side by scented Miracle cyclamen (**below**). For an even more striking effect use the dramatic coloured ornamental cabbages but, be warned, they're not for the faint hearted!

How about this pastel yellow spring display which is also delightfully fragrant (**above**). It's rather clever as the bulbs have been bought in flower and plunged into the window box behind the primroses and ivy to create a beautiful backdrop. When the bulbs finish flowering they are lifted out and replaced with pots of flowering white or yellow tulips. It's instant gardening, expensive but very effective.

Choosing Window Boxes

Just like other containers, window boxes are made in a variety of materials.
Each with their own pro's and con's...

Choosing a Box

Size matters! The wider and deeper it is, the more compost it will hold so it won't dry out as quickly (and that means less watering, hooray). Also, plants develop bigger root systems in larger window boxes, so they usually grow better.

As a rule of thumb, choose a window-box with a minimum depth and width of 20cm/8in. The length of the window-box can be important too. If you are positioning it just beneath a windowsill, it will look best if it's just slightly shorter than the length of the sill.

Terracotta:
Lovely though they are, they may not be the best choice as they can be heavy and the smaller sizes can dry out very quickly.

Wood:
The beauty of wooden window boxes is that you can make them (or if you're as bad at DIY as me, get them made!) to any size you like. Painted or stained in the colour of your choice, they can be made (or bought) sleek and modern or solid and traditional to fit your look and style.

Wooden window boxes will slowly deteriorate in time as the sides and base are in constant contact with moist compost. To minimise the problem, line the insides with a polythene sheet before planting, but do make a series of drainage holes in the bottom layer to allow water to drain away. One crafty way around the problem is to plant up a plastic window-box and place it inside a wooden window-box. So you get the best of both worlds, the look of wood with the longevity of plastic.

Plastic:
I've been tempted by some incredibly inexpensive window boxes in garden centres but I've usually resisted the urge to buy them as the really cheap ones tend to crack easily. If your budget permits, pay a little more for better quality version and look for one with a thick, solid rim which makes it easier to handle after planting up.

What a beautifully planted window box! Note the feet at the base which help any excess water drain away easily.

Fixing Window Boxes

❀ Window boxes can be very heavy so it's really important to secure them properly. Make sure you do this before you plant it up as full boxes make the job twice as difficult.

❀ **For boxes on windowsills:** **Most windowsills slope slightly, so place a couple of chocks under the box to level it. This not only helps prevent the box from slipping off but also lets the water drain away more easily. For absolute security, fix it in place with a couple of angle brackets attached to the sill or side of the window or wire it in using eye hooks connected to window frame or wall.**

❀ **For boxes beneath windowsills:** Buy a pair of window box brackets from a garden centre. They have a lip on them that prevents the box from slipping off. When positioning the brackets, the top of the box should be at least 5cm/2in below the window ledge, any higher and you might block the drip channel on the underside of most sills. If you have side-opening windows, or if you are planning to grow extra tall plants that could block light from the room, lower the box even further. The brackets should be positioned so that the weight of the box is evenly distributed, leaving an overlap of 10cm/4in at each end. For extra security, you could attach the box to the brackets with galvanised wire.

❀ **For boxes on railings: You can buy special sturdy metal brackets which hook onto railings and hold the box safely and securely.**

Growing Success

Part of the enjoyment of window boxes is that, once you've mastered the basics, they are easier to care for than hanging baskets. Here's what you need to do.

Planting Up

Water your plants first. Then cover the bottom of the box with a 2.5cm/1in layer of broken bits of pot or polystyrene (making sure that the drainage holes are covered so that they don't get blocked with compost).

Loosely fill the box with compost (ordinary multi-purpose compost is ideal, plus Container Magic, see page 58, for an easy care window box) to within 2.5cm/1in of the rim, then remove the plants from their pots. Plant the back of the window-box first and then work forward. Make a hole for each plant and place them at the same level as they were in the pot, firming the compost around them. Water in with a diluted fertiliser.

After Care

From then on, as with any container, it's important to water and feed regularly (see my tips on page 58). Remove any dead flowers and if any of the trailing plants get a bit straggly or over-dominant, then simply cut them back to size.

Top: A feast of herbs growing in a plastic window box that has been placed inside a slatted wooden frame.

Bottom: Pansies and lettuce create a colourful combination in this fibre clay window box.

Far right: You get the feeling that this stately window box has been here for centuries. Magnificent!

Choosing Plants

When I first planted up containers, I gingerly began by popping a few summer bedding plants in pots in sunny spots on the patio. Encouraged by the results, I became slightly bolder and started to use containers more creatively. A few disasters soon taught me the importance of choosing the right plants for the right place.

In my early stages of container gardening, I was given a pot of lemon verbena and was astounded by the incredible fragrance of its leaves. Ever since then I've enjoyed growing aromatic and scented plants in pots and never fail to grow something fragrant every summer. Over the years, I've also become a bit bolder with my colour combinations in pots and baskets, some work beautifully, others less so (it's a bit like my dress sense according to my family). So I was really pleased when David Ponton kindly agreed to share his tips to make colour really work. I hope that this chapter inspires you to make even more of your containers.

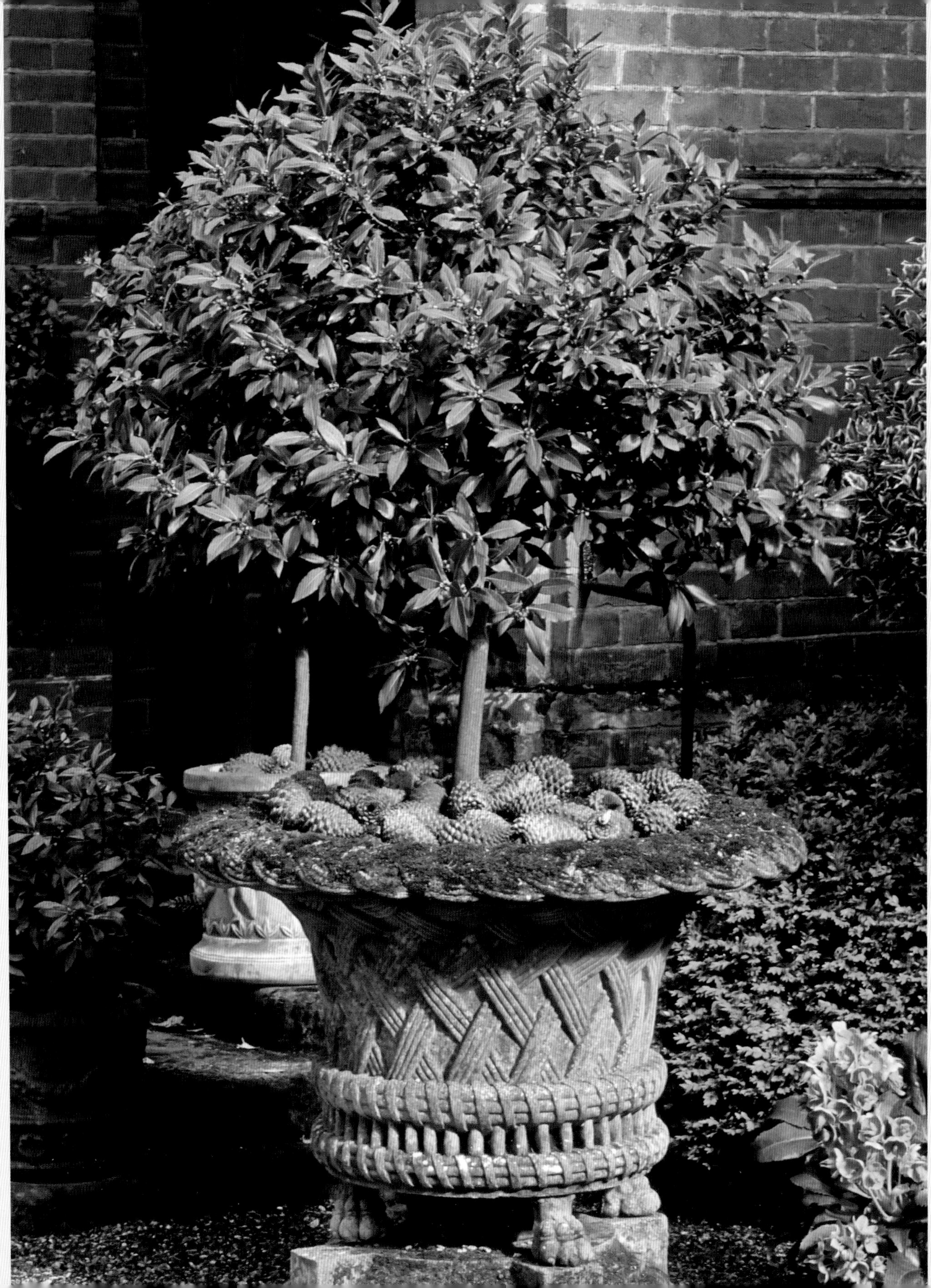

Year Round Impact

For show-stopping colour, you can't beat bedding plants and bulbs. But their display will be over by the end of the season and have to be replaced. Perennial plants can provide structure, interest and some colour all year. But if you combine perennials with bedding and bulbs, you can get the best of both worlds!

Pop an evergreen plant like euonymus or small conifer in the centre of a hanging basket or pot, together with some pretty small leaved variegated ivies around the edge, and fill the gaps with summer bedding. Then at the end of the summer, when you'd normally empty everything out, you leave the perennials in place and replace the summer bedding with winter pansies which provide a splash of colour all the way through to the end of May.

❀ Some evergreen plants are so striking that they can simply be planted in pots on their own and they'll create year round structure and interest on the patio. I love clipped box, especially the box balls. They look amazing, even in the depths of winter. Bamboo and evergreen grasses look wonderful too. Their leaves sway gently in the breeze, creating ripples of colour and movement that add extra charm and interest to the patio.

❀ Smaller plants, like English lavender can create year round impact too. The secret with these is to clip them back hard immediately after flowering so they create a beautiful mound of silver foliage that looks stunning, even in winter.

❀ Japanese maples are fabulous too. They're not evergreen, but the elegantly shaped bare branches look enchanting in winter and you can't say that about

Above: Japanese maples add a touch of grace to the patio all year round.

Far left: Evergreen plants, like bay, can provide structure as well as style through all the seasons.

many plants! In spring and summer when in leaf, they look even more beautiful and In autumn the leaves turn mouthwatering shades of red and gold. I adore the cut leaved maples (Acer palmatum dissectum which has green filigree leaves, A.p.d. atropurpureum has purple), both grow, very slowly, to 1.2m/4ft. Best grown in a sheltered spot, in partial shade and kept well watered, as strong winds, very hot sun and dry conditions can cause the delicate leaves to turn brown at the edges.

Winter Colour

When the summer show is fading and frosts threaten, most gardeners empty their pots and baskets, and store them away for winter. Give them a new lease of life by filling them with plants that will delight you from autumn through to spring.

Not only that, autumn planted containers need very little care. A little dead-heading, the occasional watering if the weather is exceptionally dry, and that's about it. There's no need to feed until the spring, and even pests are scarce in the winter. Nothing could be easier and while winter containers will never be quite as colourful as summer displays, they are incredibly cheering, even on the most miserable winter's day. One tip, plant generously as little growth will be made until the spring so plant much more densely than you would a summer basket and use bigger plants to give instant impact.

✿ For the simplest colour, plant pots and baskets with just one colour of winter flower pansy (**'Matrix'**, ideally) or the even tougher, but smaller flowered violas. For a slightly more sophisticated look, plant two complimentary colours such as lemon and white (a fresh, cool look) or burnt orange and bright red for a fiery combination.

✿ Much as I love spring flowering bulbs in pots, they do look a bit boring until they flower. But if you plant them with some winter interest such as pansies, the pots and baskets can look colourful through the winter (and they'll keep the colour going through the spring too, when the bulbs have finished blooming). For the best effect, plant one colour of bulb with one colour of bedding, ie pink tulips with blue pansies.

✿ If you visit the garden centre in the autumn, you'll find lots of really pretty foliage plants that can add extra colour to winter pots and baskets. I particularly like using the trailing plants that soften the edges of the planters especially small leaved ivy (sold in all colours from plain green to white or gold variegated), the golden leaved form of lysimachia (creeping jenny), lamium and ajuga. Look out for mound forming evergreen herbs too, such as golden thyme.

Left: Winter flowering pansies are invaluable for months of colour.

Right: Skimmia and Christmas cherry (Solanum) create some warming colour in this winter planter. When the cherry finishes it can be replaced with spring flowering plants.

Choosing Plants for Scent

Fragrant plants are like living aromatherapy – they just make you feel better. Some scents are strong and powerful, others are more subtle and are only obvious in the evening. But all of them add to the enjoyment of the garden.

So when planning your pots and baskets for colour and impact, try to add some fragrant plants too. Hang a basket of purple petunias close to your favourite seat, grow sweet peas in tubs, cottage garden pinks in pots close to the house so that their clove fragrance can waft indoors. Make the most of plants with scented leaves, such as herbs and lavender, too. Just gently brush the foliage to release their delicious perfume. Whatever plant you're growing, their perfume will be more intense if you place your pots and baskets in sunny spots.

✿ I just love growing lilies in pots. Despite their exotic appearance, they're amongst the easiest of all plants to grow in pots (for growing tips, see page 104). However, while all lilies are beautiful, not all are fragrant so choose with care! My favourites to grow in pots for scent are pure white **'Casa Blanca'**, deep orange–yellow **'Golden Splendour'**, deep rose **'Pink Perfection'** and crimson pink **'Star Gazer'**.

✿ Some daffodils are delightfully fragrant too. **'Minnow'** is a multi-flowered miniature marvel, growing just 15cm/6in high, with perfumed, rounded, creamy yellow petals with a lemon cup. For slightly larger pots and tubs, try sweetly scented **'Thalia'** with milky white flowers on 30cm/12in stems. The 'pheasant's eye' narcissus, **'Actea'** is slightly taller, at 40cm/16in, but stunning in a spot sheltered from the wind. It has glistening white petals with a golden, red-rimmed eye,

Lilium 'Casa Blanca'

and a scent that is almost as rich as a lily! For maximum impact, grow against a plain green background.

✿ Scented leaf geraniums are brilliant plants – tough, trouble free and fast growing (even in light shade). Like other aromatic leaved plants, they're best placed where you can brush against them to release their strong aromatic fragrances. There's quite a variety to choose from including lemon, peppermint, pine, cedar and roses. Just sniff a few at the garden centre before deciding. Although they don't flower anywhere near as prolifically as bedding geraniums, the blooms are pretty and they can be used in cooking too.

Making the Most of Colour

DAVID PONTON – *Hayloft Plants*

Have you ever wondered why some containers look so much better than others? The colours just look so good together. Some lucky people have a natural flair for colour combinations but the rest of us can create similar stunning effects by using something that Sir Isaac Newton discovered a few centuries ago! It's called a colour wheel and it consists of twelve sections, each of a different colour. The great scientist's original colour wheel has since been updated to create a more modern version which is the one I prefer to use.

Anyone can use this clever colour wheel to create combinations of colours which always look good together. So when I'm choosing flower colours I use these tips (Sir Isaac called them laws) to create amazing looking containers.

Opposite Colours

The colour you choose and its opposite, make each other dazzle! Essentially, the 'candlepower' of both colours is boosted. For container gardeners this is the most dramatic of all laws, because it allows us to bring out the best in certain plants.

In the illustration on the right you'll see how I chose a rich violet-blue and found its opposite in a pale yellow. Now look at the photo on page 77 to see how I've used this in a container planting in my garden. You can see how I combined the deep-violet blue of my Anchusa with the pale yellow of a Verbascum to create an eye-catching combination. Individually, both are superb plants, but together they look even more striking. So, to really brighten up any container, simply pick opposite colours on the colour wheel. It works a treat every time.

Newton's original colour wheel

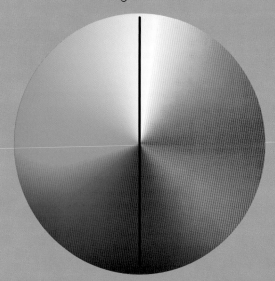

Modern version of the colour wheel with shading

Above: Opposite colours look fabulous. Choose any point on the colour wheel and draw a line through the centre to find its opposite.

Adjoining Colours

Alternatively, try combining colours from two of the adjoining sections. Choose any section, then move either one section clockwise, or one section anti-clockwise. With the modern wheel you just move the same distance.

In this example (**below**), I've decided to choose a lilac and pink display for a pot. Any colours within the line will look wonderful together. For best effect, don't use more than three different varieties of plants.

To fit the colours from my line into the planting, my first two choices are a purple Cineraria senetti and a lilac Cineraria senetti. With the lilac Cineraria there is a touch of white, (whites, greys or black are neutral colours and can be combined with any of the other colours).

My third choice of plant is a pink Argyranthemum – again from the same line on my colour wheel. I like the simplicity of this display and the fact it is in a grey container (which of course is another neutral colour). You can see on the opposite page how good this looks.

Triangulated Colours

You can also combine the two preceding ideas for amazing effects. Choose one of the twelve segments and join two segments with a line. The line you have drawn, forms the short base of a triangle. Now complete the triangle by drawing the two long sides. It is the shades around the three points of the triangle which makes for great design.

These colours will work superbly together and once you have understood 'The Triangle' you are on the way to becoming a prize-winning gardener, a fashion guru or even an interior designer!

The container in the photo on the next page is based on the triangle illustrated below. Taking the yellow and orange segment part of the wheel, this planting contains a dwarf sunflower, a calandula and a nasturtium (note – three plants again). You can see these are the colours around the two points on the short side of the triangle.

However this is not what makes this so intriguing.

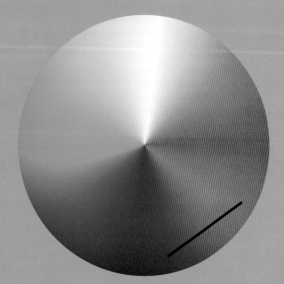

Adjoining colours on the colour wheel

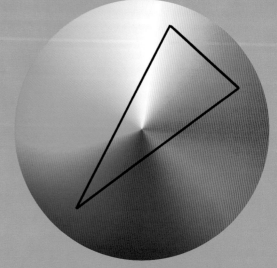

Triangulated colours on the colour wheel

Opposite colours

Adjoining colours

Triangulated colours

Look at the colour of the container! It's been chosen using the colour around the point where the long sides of the triangle meet. To me this is quite superb because the designer has used the Law of Triangle, not only in plant selection, but in choosing the right BLUE colour for the container! What a super look this has created.

Newton's colour wheel is the secret behind many great designers. And it can help anyone, from beginner to expert gardener, create some fantastic looking containers.

David Ponton was originally an osteopath specialising in spinal disorders in racehorses and he took up gardening after a life-threatening injury. I really love his wonderful enthusiasm and passion for plants, and always learn something new from him, especially when he reveals the fascinating history and stories behind Hayloft Plants.

Best Plants *for* Containers

With so many wonderful plants to choose from, it has been quite a challenge picking the plants for this section. I've made a very personal selection of what I consider to be the very best plants for pots, baskets and window boxes. Many are tried and trusted favourites but I've also included some of the very latest plants that have recently proven themselves in growing trials.

Regular viewers of QVC will know that our gardening guests include some world leading experts. As I began writing this book, I talked to a number of them about their experiences of growing their specialist plants in containers. What they told me was so interesting that I asked them if I could feature their personal comments. They very kindly agreed and I'm delighted to include their knowledge and expertise in this section.

Best Bedding Plants

Bedding is a handy catch-all term for a whole range of plants that give wonderful colour and form to both winter and summer containers. They're the ones that you plant fresh each year to give your pots that wow factor.

Some are annuals, like lobelia, whilst many others, such as fuchsias are tender perennials. I've even included a few hardy perennials because, as young plants, they look really good in seasonal plantings. Where relevant, I've included the spread as well as the height of the plant.

Argyranthemum (Marguerites):

Fantastic performers for sunny positions. I like growing these in containers on their own where they create wonderful domes of fern-like leaves covered with beautiful daisy-like flowers. Pinch out the main shoots on young plants to create bushier plants with more

Bacopa 'Snowflake'

blooms. Need regular deadheading to keep them at their best. Look out for RHS trial toppers, **'White Beauty'** and **'Sultan's Lemon'** (40x40cm/16x16in).

Bacopa: A gem for hanging baskets and pots for full sun or part shade. It spreads as well as trails, so you get double your money's worth! The traditional variety **'Snowflake'** (trails 45cm/18in) has fresh green leaves and masses of small, pure white single flowers but is destined to be surpassed soon by larger white flowered forms. There are some excellent new Double flowered and blue forms about to be introduced too.

Begonias: If you had to choose just one bedding plant, this is it! They are easy, reliable in any weather, in any position, produce an amazing display and some are scented too. For mini-domes of colour (and as a replacement for the poor old disease hit busy lizzie), grow the semperflorens varieties (choose between the **'Devil'** range with stunning dark leaves, the **'Heaven'** range with shiny green leaves or **'Organdy'** which has a mix of both). I also love the Non-Stop begonias with their strong, bright and eye-catching colours but the amazing new **'Peardrops'** and **'Buffy'** varieties are even better (45x45cm/18x18in). The trailing forms of begonias are just as mouthwatering. **'Apricot Shades'** is, deservedly, the bestseller, a stunner that produces an incredible display of colour in beautiful shades of apricot, yellow and gold (trails 38cm/15in). At the end of the summer, each plant also produces a tuber which

Begonia 'Apricot Shade'

Begonia 'Organdy' Mixed

Begonia 'Peardrops'

you can save and grow on for an even prettier display the following year. I know of some gardeners who have saved their 'Apricot Shades' tubers for 8 years on the trot. Other good trailers include the striking, extra long flowering **'Million Kisses'** and **'Dragon Wings'** (trailing 45cm/18in).

Diascia and Nemesia: Superb patio and basket plant that produce masses of pretty, small flowers all summer. They grow especially well in our climate and are surprisingly drought tolerant. Clip them back in early August and they'll rebound with renewed vigour. One plant can easily fill a 30cm/12in pot. Look out for Diascia **'Little'** range. Nemesia is similar but the **'Aromatica'** range is scented. Last summer, I saw an amazing display of a row of identical pots leading up to the entrance of a posh hotel. Each was filled with a single planting of blue nemesias. It looked simply stunning.

Gazania: Large, showy daisy like flowers in a range of cheery colours, from deep orange to yellow. They flower all summer long in a sunny spot on spreading bushes about 30cm/1ft high. As the flowers face upwards, plant in pots on the patio or low level baskets and boxes, so you can enjoy their full beauty. Incredibly drought tolerant **'Tiger Stripes'** is one of the best selections – and my dad's favourite too!

Lobelia: Much loved for their summer display. The traditional seed raised forms hate drying out, they have to be kept well watered otherwise they may stop flowering. In trials last summer, I was very impressed with the new cutting raised varieties which flower even better, even longer and they're more tolerant of lapses in watering. **'Superstar'** is an upright form, while **'Waterfall Blue Ice'** and the **'Hot'** varieties are trailing.

Gazania 'Tiger Stripes'

Lobelia 'Superstar'

Osteospermum 'Serenity'

Petunia 'Express Patriot' Mixed

Osteospermum: Don't let the name put you off (it sounds like a dreadful disease!). I prefer the common name, Cape Daisies, and they're a cracking choice for containers, producing masses of large, daisy like flowers with a silky sheen. The bush forms are best known, pick the **'Serenity'** range (30cm/12in), or the amazing long flowering **'Voltage Yellow'**. The new trailing form, **'Sunbrella'** (which trails 45cm/18in) is superb, use a mix of colours for the best looking baskets.

Petunia: Superstars of the gardening world. And they're getting better and better! For traditional bush petunias, growing about 30cm/12in high, pick from the **'Express'** range and plant a single colour per pot for the most dramatic impact. Of the trailing petunias, Surfinias are the best known, Blue and Hot Pink are the biggest selling colours, and they give a fantastic display (trailing to 1.5m/5ft. However I find they can get a little straggly later in the season which is one the reasons why I prefer the **'Fanfare'** range (which hugs the basket with a 90cm/3ft ball of flowers). The double flowered **'Tumbelina'** petunias (trail 45cm/18in) are gorgeous and, as a bonus, some have a fine fragrance, especially **'Joanna'**. **Callibrachoas** (another mouthful of a name) are trailing forms of mini-petunias and they're ideal for smaller containers or baskets where ordinary trailing petunias would over-dominate. The **'Cabaret'** range (trail 20cm/8in) produces masses of fifty pence sized flowers and is more tolerant of poor conditions than other mini-petunias.

Sunpatiens: One of the most exciting new plants for years! It's like a giant busy lizzie (but, unlike ordinary busy lizzies, is resistant to the downy mildew disease that has devastated these much loved plants recently). Sunpatiens grow three times the size of standard busy lizzies, produces three times the number of flowers, and has three times the root system. Grow it as a showstopper in big pots (where it can reach 45x45cm/ 18x18in) or as the centre piece in a basket. A cracker and highly recommended.

Geraniums: For maximum colour, with minimum effort, grow geraniums, the stars of the summer show. They really are remarkable plants, flowering their hearts out all season long, and unlike fuchsias, which can be slightly diva like and a bit demanding, they are down to earth performers who can survive incredible amounts of neglect. They can happily cope with being dried out for several days, bouncing back to health when you finally water them again.

Just before I continue, I ought to clear up one confusion. They should really be called pelargoniums, the name they were first given 200 years ago, to distinguish them from the true geraniums which are hardy garden plants. But Queen Victoria, amongst others, started calling them geraniums and the name stuck, and that's what most people (apart from the botanists) know them as.

The bush varieties, with large globes of flowers and rounded, slightly scalloped leaves (often with a maroon, horseshoe shape pattern hence their name 'Zonal' geraniums) are perfect as a centrepiece for any container or basket, producing a fantastic display of flowers from the minute you put them out, right through until the first frosts. Those with double or semi-double flowers are the showiest, but tend to catch and hold the rain so can rot in wet weather. The singles have fewer petals but produce more flower heads, so are just as colourful and completely rainproof.

Breeders are forever introducing new ranges (series) of plants, but generally anything you choose will do you proud. Simply pick the colour you like. Cutting

Geranium 'Maverick'

Geranium 'Sybil'

How to Take Geranium Cuttings

✿ Geraniums root quickly and easily from cuttings. I like to take them in late July. Select 10cm/4in non-flowering side-shoots, trim just beneath the node (leaf joint), remove the lower leaves and insert them in individual 7.5cm/3in pots or in compact root-trainers, using a mix of multipurpose compost and grit (or perlite). Keep in a warm, light spot and water very moderately.

Pinch out the growing tips of new shoots to keep the plants bushy.

Keep these young rooted plants indoors on a light windowsill over winter and they'll grow into big, flowering size plants for the following summer. You can also use these over-wintered plants to produce an extra batch of cuttings in March. Taken then, each will grow into sturdy young plants by May.

Seed raised geraniums plug plants ready for potting on.

raised plants (normally sold in small pots) tend to be more expensive than seed raised geraniums but have more, bigger and better flowers. If pushed, for a double flowered form, I'd pick the PAC range, especially the brick red **'Octavia Hill'** or the **Designer** range which has huge heads of flowers, up to 15cm/6in across. Seed raised geraniums are usually sold in packs of 4 or 6, the **'Maverick'** or **'Horizon'** ranges are the most popular.

To cascade down the side of baskets and containers, the trailing or ivy-leaved forms are unbeatable for trouble-free colour and impact. I love and really recommend the **'Sybil'** range trail 45cm/18in), whose flowers look like miniature roses that open up in the prettiest posies of flowers. The lilac pink is the best of these colours. Recently, a new selection of Swiss balcon type trailing geranium has been introduced, called **'Gerainbow'** (trail 60cm/2ft). These are incredibly weatherproof and easy to grow.

All geraniums do best in full sun and are tender perennials, so bring them indoors to overwinter before the first frosts. It's also very easy to take cuttings (see page 85) and is a great way to increase your stocks of these lovely plants (for free).

Fuchsias: If you're looking for sheer, breathtaking glamour, fuchsias are unbeatable. The gorgeous, dancing flowers, either in single or the more showy double forms, provide a spectacular display of colour from summer to the first frosts. But they do need a little cosseting. Their most important requirement is moist compost: if it dries out the flowers and buds will usually fall off, and it can take six weeks for the plant to recover. So it's essential to water them regularly, especially if they're in a hot sunny position. Many gardeners prefer to grow them in light shade where they'll be just as happy and will need less watering. For best results with fuchsias, pinch out the growing tips

Fuchsia 'Flower Fairy Ice'

Fuchsia 'Swingtime'

when planting to encourage strong, dense growth.

Bush fuchsias make dramatic centrepieces for hanging baskets and window-boxes. Grown in pots, the down-turned flowers are hard to enjoy in their full glory unless you can raise them up to eye level. There are some really superb varieties available, and in a wide range of colour combinations. My top choices are the **Flower Fairy** range (which is half hardy) and crimson/ purple **'Jolly Nantes'** (50cm/20in) and **'Beckie-Lou'** (120cm/4ft bush or grow as a half-standard) both of which are hardy so can be left outside in a sheltered spot over-winter to grow on the next year.

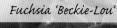

Fuchsia 'Voodoo'

Fuchsia 'Beckie-Lou'

Fuchsia 'Buds of May'

Trailing Fuchsias: As for the trailing forms, use them to cascade down the side of your containers. Again, the range is terrific, and some of the best include white and red **'Swingtime'** and cerise purple **'Dollar Princess'** (trail up to 45cm/18in). The **'Buds of May'** range is also good as they flower up to 4 weeks earlier than traditional varieties and keep on blooming until the first frosts. For maximum impact, look out for the giant flowered varieties like red and blue **'Voodoo'** with huge double flowers up to 10cm/4in across. You don't get quite as many flowers compared with ordinary trailing doubles, they don't trail quite as much (to 30cm/12in) and they are slightly less tolerant of poor weather, but boy do they make up for it with their size. These are the flowers that will knock the socks off your friends and neighbours.

The majority of bedding fuchsias are tender perennials, so if you want to keep them for next year, you'll have to over-winter them indoors in a frost-free spot. Cuttings can be taken at almost any time, but are easiest in midsummer.

Other Favourites of Mine

Marigolds: Bright and brash, you either love or hate them but they flower brilliantly all summer and brighten up the dullest of days. Pick **'Zenith'** or **'Bonanza'**.

Rudbeckia: Terrific performers in pots, especially **'Tiger Eye'** (50x40cm/20x16in). Creates an amazing impact from mid-summer to the first frosts. **'Cherry Brandy'** and **'Prairie Sun'** are great, too.

Verbena: I love the gloriously colourful trailing varieties that produce so many tiny flowers that they hide the leaves. **'Aztec Magic'** is my favourite.

Rudbeckia 'Tiger Eye'

Verbena 'Aztec' Mixed

Pansy 'Matrix' Mixed

Viola 'Floral Power'

Zinnia: Beautiful, long flowering, vibrant colours, and great for cutting too. The **'Zahara'** range is sold in single as well as slightly taller (35x35cm/14x14in), and just as pretty, double flowered forms.

Autumn, Winter and Spring Bedding

Pansies and Violas: The stars of winter and spring containers! They are also sold as summer bedding plants, but they struggle in the heat so are, in my opinion, a poor option for the warmer months. But, for the rest of the year, they are simply fantastic!

The best known winter pansies are the **'Universal'** range, but **'Matrix'** (20cm/8in) is a better choice as it produces bushier plants with more flowers. They start flowering in the autumn, carry on through mild spells in the winter and burst into a magnificent show of colour from the first warm days of spring through until May.

Violas (20cm/8in) have much smaller flowers, but lots more of them, and I think they are delightful. They're best in pots or baskets that can be admired up close. The **'Floral Power'** range of violas is the most highly regarded, they've real charm and flower for as many months as the best of the winter pansies. Recently, a new lightly scented trailing pansy has been introduced, appropriately named **'Plentifall'** (trails 45cm/18in).

All winter pansies and violas can be grown in sun or shade but need to be kept well watered. Regular deadheading and feeding (in the spring) helps produce the best display. If you're growing plants from plugs, buy early so you can pot them on in August to produce well sized plants before the onset of winter.

Polyanthus and Primroses: Along with pansies and violas, polyanthus are the showiest of spring flowering plants. The flowers are held in clusters on tall stems and the best range, **'Crescendo'** grows to 30cm/1ft. It's completely winter hardy, producing its first flowers extra early (from mid winter, if it's mild) and it's sold in a wonderful choice of rainbow like colours. Primroses produce rosettes of flowers, most varieties aren't as hardy as polyanthus so they are best bought as flowering size plants in the spring, once the weather warms up, and popped into containers as instant colour. For totally winter hardy varieties, ask for **'Wanda'**, **'Husky'** or **'Alaska'**, all can be grown outside in winter and will flower from early spring onwards.

Cyclamen: If you're looking for a splash of autumn colour, these are delightful. The **'Miracle'** cyclamen look like miniature versions of the indoor favourites, with the same beautifully patterned leaves and enchanting fragrant flowers (salmon shades have the most scent). I plant some up every autumn and put them on our covered, outdoor porch and they cheer me up for months. Sadly, they only last until mid-December but I enjoy every minute of them.

> **"If you're growing pansy or primula plants from plugs, buy early so you can pot them up in August to produce well sized plants before the onset of winter."**

Polyanthus 'Crescendo'

Cyclamen 'Miracle'

Other Favourites of Mine

Chrysanthemum: **'Showmaker Improved'**
are breathtaking. Each plant can produce a huge dome,
45x45cm/18x18in, covered with over 100 flowers.
They look stunning from mid-August to early October.
Grow these from young, plug sized plants bought in the
spring or buy as big pots of instant colour in the late
summer. Plant in the garden after flowering for years
more colour.

Herbs: Yes, you can use them as bedding plants!
Garden Centres sell small pots of the prettiest evergreen
herbs, like variegated or golden thyme, in the autumn.
These add a lovely splash of colour (and fragrance) to
winter pots and baskets. When you empty the container
in late spring, pop the herbs into bigger pots and grow
them on for summer harvesting.

Trailing plants: There's a surprising range of
small, colourful evergreen trailing plants that can be
used in winter containers. I love ivy, especially the
small leaved silver forms like **'Glacier'**. The golden
Lysimachia (creeping jenny) is especially colourful,
as is **Lamium 'White Nancy'** (glowing, green edged
silver leaves) and **'Gold Nuggets'** (bright gold with a
silver flash). At the end of the season, pop them all into
bigger pots or plant in the garden.

Chrysanthemum 'Showmaker Improved'

Lamium 'White Nancy'

My Favourite Bedding Plants

Paul Hansord – *Thompson & Morgan*

With over 40 years of growing and assessing literally thousands of different varieties of plants it is not easy to select my favourites. However, after careful consideration, here are the varieties I would grow if I was shipped off to my desert island! Interestingly, only two varieties have been available for over 30 years and, therefore, my list unwittingly demonstrates what a wonderful job the plant breeders have done on improving the performance of plants in our gardens.

My Personal Choice

Climbing Fuchsia 'Lady Boothby' or **'Lady in Black':** Both of these Fuchsia's grow vigorously and are perfect for covering frames and making a distinct feature on the patio.

Petunia F1 Hybrid 'Tidal Wave' Mixed: This multiflora Petunia grows vigorously and will cascade down 60–90cm/2–3ft in a hanging basket or will grow to 1.5m/5ft tall on a climbing frame. This seed raised Petunia has flowers that are the most resistant to wet weather.

Sweet Pea 'Sweet Dreams': You will get absolutely amazing scents for weeks on end, as long as you keep cutting the flowers.

Begonia 'Apricot Shades Improved' or **'Apricot Fragrant Falls':** My favourite plant for hanging baskets, both varieties produce a cascade of orange, apricot picotee flowers whatever the British summer throws at us!

Marigold F1 Hybrid 'Zenith' Mixed: This very pretty variety does not set seed and therefore produces masses of large yellow, golden flowers until the first frost.

Patio Gerbera: If you are looking for a plant to impress your neighbours this is the variety for you. Suitable for growing on the patio and will produce 13cm/5in flowers by the dozen throughout the season, if kept frost free it will be even more spectacular the following summer.

Fuchsia 'Jolly Nantes': This recently bred variety is the most floriferous Fuchsia that I know of and, as I write, was still flowering in November in my garden.

Sunpatiens: One of the more expensive patio plants and is tolerant of downy mildew but the giant flowers and vigour of the plant means that you only have to plant one instead of three ordinary Busy Lizzies.

Pinks 'Tropical Butterfly': Unique flower colours on plants that will flower for weeks in the garden or that will last for 3 weeks as a cut flower.

Climbing Fuchsia 'Lady Boothby'

Sweet Pea 'Sweet Dreams'

Petunia F1 Hybrid 'Tidal Wave'

Marigold F1 Hybrid 'Zenith'

Patio Gerbera

Fuchsia 'Jolly Nantes'

Sunpatiens

Pinks 'Tropical Butterfly'

My Growing Tips

❀ If you're planning to grow on plug plants for your containers, order them early so they are delivered early and you can grow them on properly before planting them out. The earlier you order in the season, the bigger and better your plants will grow so you can enjoy a longer flowering period as well as lots more flowers.

❀ **When growing plug plants, encourage them to bush out by pinching out the main shoot above 4 to 5 leaves (right). Side shoots will then develop and for even better plants, pinch out their main shoots once another 4 to 5 leaves have grown.**

❀ Steel yourself and remove all flowers just before planting into containers and for the first three weeks afterwards. It may seem a bit drastic when the plant looks so nice but this will encourage the plant to make roots and establish quicker, this again will encourage more flowers through the summer.

❀ **Feeding plants, with an extra high potash plant food like Flower Power, makes a huge difference to the plant's performance. We don't perform well if we are not fed and watered and plants are no different.**

❀ Do grow your favourites but also try something different every year. New varieties are introduced all the time, and recent improvements in flower size and garden performance has been dramatic. For instance, who would have thought that the florist's Gerbera could be transformed into such an impressive new variety of patio plant. But that's just one of the latest examples of the plant breeders working their magic!

One of the main advantages of growing plants in patio pots is that you can change your display on a regular basis and really enjoy the plants when they are at their best. Follow my tips and you will have the most colourful display in your neighbourhood!

Paul's the man I turn to with my bedding plant questions. Starting his career in a garden centre, he moved to Unwins Seeds where he was responsible for running their trial grounds. He's worked for Thompson & Morgan for many years and is a top judge for the RHS. Paul travels the world finding the best new plants and is usually the first to sell them!

Best Bulbs

Bulbs are worth their weight in gold.
I just love them!

Pop spring flowering bulbs into your containers when planting in the autumn, forget about them in the winter, and once the weather warms, up they suddenly burst into growth and delight you with a glorious display of colour. At the end of the spring, it's best to re-plant them into the garden, as few spring bulbs thrive in containers from year to year (except species tulips).

I also grow lots of summer flowering bulbs (some of which are technically called corms or tubers), all of them provide a real touch of glamour for months on end. If you're pushed for space and can grow just one summer bulb, make it a lily. You just can't go wrong with them!

Spring Bulbs

Crocus: These are real gems, easy to grow and some of the most cheering sights of the early spring. They're great value for money too. For really early flowers, plant the species varieties such as the elegant, pale yellow **'Cream Beauty'**, or rich, deep violet **'Ruby Giant'** (7.5cm/3in). The Dutch hybrids bloom are bigger, flower slightly later but are less prone to mice and squirrels digging them up.

Hyacinths: Hyacinths provide a breathtaking spectacle in April, and an equally breathtaking scent. To maximum impact, plant several bulbs per pot, all the same colour (as different colours flower at different times). Growing to 25cm/10in, the heavy flowerheads can snap in strong winds, so choose a sheltered spot.

Crocus 'Cream Beauty'

Iris reticulata 'Harmony'

Muscari 'Azureum'

Narcisus 'Rijnveld's Early Sensation'

'White Carnegie' and **'Delft Blue'** are two of my favourites, whilst **'Woodstock'**, a gorgeous, deep royal purple, is outstanding. All hyacinths are equally good in sun or partial shade.

Iris: Spring Iris are amongst the most delightful of small bulbs, flowering as early as February. The sweetly scented yellow danfordiae grows to only 10cm/4in, whilst the slightly taller 'reticulata' varieties (15cm/6in) cover virtually every shade of blue – sky blue **'Harmony'** and deep rich purple **'George'** are amongst the most desirable. Ideal companions with other plants, they look best planted in clumps rather than dotted around.

Muscari: Most gardeners know the common grape hyacinth Muscari armenaicum which is fine in pots but not as good when planted in the garden later (it's almost weed like and produces more leaves than flowers). Pick the much more desirable **'Azureum'** with tightly packed powder blue flowers (8cm/5in) or the stunning **'Latifolium'** (15cm/6in), a beautiful two tone flower, blackish blue at the bottom but bright blue on top.

Daffodil (Narcissus): Daffodils are a sheer delight, the one indispensible spring bulb. They're tough, reliable, and unbeatable for their colourful display which usually peaks in March. Dwarf varieties are perfect for pots, baskets and window-boxes, and there are some stunners to choose from. For the earliest flowers (even in January), the pure yellow **'Rijnveld's Early Sensation'** (25cm/10in) is always stunning. Other favourites are **'February Gold'** (30cm/12in) which normally flowers in March!, deep golden yellow multi-flowered **'Tete a Tete'** (15cm/6in), the lesser known but fabulous **'Jack Snipe'** with a deep primrose trumpet set off by pearly white petals (22cm/9in). I also love primrose yellow **'Minnow'** (30cm/12in) which needs to be admired close up to see its real beauty. In larger pots, in a sheltered position where the stems won't be buffeted by wind, April flowering **'Geranium'** (35cm/14in) with multiple heads of white, orange/red cupped scented flowers is a beauty. And the scented May flowering **'Actea'** (40cm/16in), with its fluttering white petals and tiny red-rimmed 'eye' is simply fabulous and many gardener's absolute favourite.

Narcisus 'Februaury Gold'

Narcisus 'Minnow'

Narcisus 'Geranium'

Narcisus 'Tete a Tete'

Tulipa 'Spring Green'

Tulipa 'China Pink'

Tulipa 'Showwinner'

Tulipa 'Pink Dwarf'

Tulipa batalinii 'Bronze Charm'

Tulipa Linifolia

Tulips: For a magnificent long lasting display, these are possibly the finest and certainly showiest of all spring bulbs. There's a tulip to suit everyone, in a glorious range of colours and styles, from the quietly simple to the outrageous show-offs like the parrot tulips. Heights vary tremendously and the really tall varieties, growing over 60cm/2ft are generally better planted in the garden rather than in pots. Pick your bulbs according to their height (to suit your container) and pick them for a succession of colour. Amongst the best of the smaller types are the March flowering kaufmanniana types such as the scarlet red **'Showwinner'** (22cm/9in) which has attractively marked leaves too. In pots on their own, try the deep apricot batalinii **'Bronze Charm'** (25cm/10in) and crimson red linifolia, both flowering in May. Taller, and just as choice are early April flowering **'Purissima'** (45cm/18in) which opens primrose, turns cream then goes white, mid-April blooming orange/red and scented **'Princess Irene'** and the sumptuous **'China Pink'** both 35cm/14in. For May colour, I love peony flowered pink **'Angelique'** and all time favourite pale apple white **'Spring Green'** (both around 40cm/16in).

> **"For a magnificent long lasting display these are possibly the finest and certainly the showiest of all spring bulbs."**

Summer Bulbs

Agapanthus: Imposing summer flowering bulbs which thrive in pots. The strap like leaves arch gracefully over the edges of the pot providing the perfect foil for the globes of blue or white bell shaped flowers from July to September. There are evergreen types, but they aren't as winter hardy as those that lose their leaves in winter. The robust **'Headbourne Hybrids'** are available in a range of shades of blue, buy in flower to get your perfect colour. Named varieties such Mid blue **'Northern Star'** and dark **'Navy Blue'** are even better (75cm/30in). Need the sunniest position possible.

Begonias: Eagle eyed readers will notice that I've also included them in the bedding plant section. They're here also since some begonias are sold as dormant tubers. For quicker impact and faster flowers in the first year, buy these instead of the young plant versions. For pots, the **'Nonstop'** varieties are reliable and the lovely dark leaved **'Mocha'** varieties are especially good and heat tolerant too. For baskets, grow illumination **'Apricot Shades'**. Save the tubers at the end of the season to grow on for the following year.

Canna: Cannas are one of the most exotic looking and striking plants that you can grow. The leaves alone are amazing, huge and paddle shaped but from midsummer, the incredible flowers appear in tropical shades of red, orange, apricot, pink or yellow. The plants grow up to 2m/6ft so they need a big tub, plenty of water and feeding. At the end of the summer, cut off the leaves, dig up the fleshy roots and store frost free over winter. It's important to only buy Cannas if they can be guaranteed as virus free stock.

Agapanthus 'Northern Star'

Begonia 'Mocha'

Canna

Dahlia 'Roxy'

Dahlias: There are fashions in plants. Dahlias have been in the wilderness for years but gardeners are suddenly re-discovering what cracking plants they can be in containers. The best are those with slightly more upright facing flowers such as golden orange **'Spanish Conquest'**, pink and white, dark leaved **'Gallery La Tour'**, magenta pink **'Roxy'** and the **'Mystic'** range. All grow 60cm/2ft or so, and are great for cutting. Keep well watered and fed, and over-winter the tubers indoors to grow for future years.

Lilies: Lilies are the stars of the summer flowering bulbs – flamboyant, colourful and remarkably easy to grow. They're perfect for pots that are at least 30cm/12in deep and you don't necessarily need many, three bulbs will provide a magnificent display in a 25cm/10in pot. The simplest to grow are the Asiatic Hybrids such as orange **'Enchantment'**, 75cm/2ft 6in but they aren't fragrant and for me, a lily has to be perfumed. For scent and beauty, I'd suggest the breathtaking pure white, huge flowered **'Casa Blanca'**, rich crimson pink and red **'Journey's End'**, and rosy pink **'Mona Lisa'** (all 90cm/3ft).

At the Chelsea Flower Show a few years ago, I spotted the incredible **'Triumphator'** which has enormous white, deep purple centred trumpet shaped flowers. It's since become an all time favourite with QVC gardeners who have sent me pictures of flowers reaching 30cm/12 across. **'Stargazer'** is the world's best selling lily, and no wonder, the crimson pink flowers spotted with maroon and edged in white, are a delight (also 30cm/12in). There are some extra dwarf varieties too, with large flowers on very short (30cm/12in) stems. They seem slightly out of proportion to me, but can suit very small spaces.

Growing Lilies in Pots

✿ If you're looking for a real show stopper for the summer patio, grow lilies. They're incredibly beautiful and surprisingly easy. Even if you've never gardened before, this is the plant to wow you, your family and your friends!

Lilies are best planted from early autumn until mid spring. When buying, pick the biggest bulbs you can buy, as bigger bulbs produce better flowers. Generally, I prefer to grow the more compact lilies, growing up to 1.2m/4ft, but taller growing lilies are also great in pots as long as you use large, heavy pots and stake the lilies so they don't fall over. You'll only need three bulbs for a 25cm/10in pot, but larger pots take five to seven bulbs (and look even more wonderful)

If you plant them in the spring, many lilies will bloom around 14 weeks from planting, Please note, it's only a guide so don't blame me if it doesn't quite work out for your special summer party!

Start off by placing some broken pieces of pot (crocks) or polystyrene chunks at the bottom of the pot, then add a couple of handfuls of compost. Plant the bulbs on top, making sure that they are then covered with around 10–15cm/4–6in of additional compost. From then on, keep the pot well watered as the bulbs grow. Feeding is also very important, as it helps the bulbs get bigger for next year's display, so feed with

You'll need to plant the bulbs fairly deep in the pot.

Lillium 'Mona Lisa'

After planting (pictured on page 104), my lilies bloomed exactly fourteen weeks later!

Flower Power or liquid tomato food regularly until September.

When the last flowers have faded remove the old flower heads, but leave as much of the stem as possible. Continue watering and feeding until the foliage and stems die back naturally in the autumn. The bulbs can be left in the pot over winter in a sheltered position outdoors.

Next spring, remove 5–7.5cm/ 2–3in of compost from the surface and replace with a fresh layer. At the end of that second summer, the bulbs may have started to get a bit congested so six to eight weeks after flowering, dig them up and replant in fresh compost in pots or the garden. Any small bulbs that have developed at the base of the stem can be grown on in separate pots. Water and feed these as normal. In the first year they may only produce wispy shoots and it can take two years or more to reach flowering size. But you'll be as proud as punch when they do!

My Favourite Bulbs

GEORGE CLOWES – *P. de Jager and Sons Limited*

I find growing bulbs in pots, hanging baskets and other containers incredibly rewarding – and essential if you only have a small garden, patio or terrace! There are so many wonderful, colourful bulbs that there is something for every type of container and all situations.

They are also incredibly versatile. I plant them on their own for dramatic focal points and use them as ornamental 'fillers' by popping in a few bulbs when planting up containers with other plants.

I always ensure that I plant several bulbs of the same variety together to make bold, vivid splashes of colour. And I also use potted bulbs as gap fillers in beds and borders. I plant them in small, plastic pots and when they come into flower, bury the pots to provide colour in otherwise bare areas.

Planting in Groups

There are so many beautiful bulb varieties available, that it is almost impossible to select a short list of my favourites – but here goes! If you try them, they will provide several months of colourful pleasure. I particularly love these tried and tested combinations. Plant the larger bulbs first, then the smaller bulbs on top.

- Fritillaria crown imperial Rubra Maxima, the most spectacular bulb with flame-orange flowers with darker veining, underplanted with Tulipa batalinii 'Bronze Charm'.
- Narcissus Tripartite, bearing two or three shining lemon-gold flowers per stem, surrounded by Muscari 'Early Giant' with deep cobalt-blue flowers.
- Tulip Kaufmanniana 'Pink Dwarf' grown with Iris reticulata Natascha.

My Personal Choice

For the most spectacular impact, I like to plant up large containers – such as a half barrel, old sink or, when I can get my hands on one, a tin bath – with a combination of different bulbs that all flower at the same time. Try these for the most wonderful displays.

Anemone blanda 'Blue Shades': I greatly admire these for their fine shades of blue flowers. Grows to 15cm/6in high.

Galanthus nivalis 'Flore Pleno': A double snowdrop with large globular blooms of peerless white with a touch of green inside, growing to 15cm/6in high.

Species tulip 'Little Beauty': Rosy-purple, with a striking deep blue centre, edged with white. Grows to 10cm/4in high.

Narcissus bulbocodium conspicuous: The yellow hoop petticoat daffodil. I love the dainty golden-yellow flowers. Grows to 15cm/6in high.

Iris reticulata Mixture: A splendid mix of colours ranging from blue to reddish-purple, all with very attractive differently coloured marked petals. Grows to 15cm/6in high.

Erythronium dens-canis 'Rose Queen': The dog's tooth violet. A splendid early-flowering variety with refined blooms of a delicate shade of clear pink. Grows to 12.5cm/5in high.

Anemone blanda 'Blue Shades'

Galanthus nivalis 'Flore Pleno'

Tulip 'Little Beauty'

Erythronium 'Rose Queen'

Iris reticulata 'George'

Chiondoxa forbesii (Glory of the Snow)

Chionodoxa forbesii (Glory of the Snow): Beautiful, bright, rich, ice-blue flowers with an almost white centre. Grows to 70–90cm/28–36in high.

My Growing Tips

✿ When buying bulbs bear in mind that bigger bulbs give much better results. Small bulbs may flower poorly or not at all.

✿ **Generally, the larger the container the better the bulbs perform, as moisture levels and temperature will not fluctuate so erratically.**

✿ When you are planting your bulbs you will need to space them so they don't touch the side of the container or each other.

✿ **Failures with bulbs are most frequently due to being planted too deeply or too shallowly. A good general rule to follow is to plant the bulb to twice its height, measuring the bulb from the base to the shoulder. So, a daffodil bulb measuring 5cm (2in) from the base to the shoulder should be planted 10cm (4in) deep.**

✿ Feeding bulbs is very important to build them up for flowering the following year. This helps encourage strong and healthy growth. Feed with a high potash fertiliser, such as Flower Power, every two to three weeks once growth has emerged, right through until after flowering, and foliage has died back.

✿ **Protect pots and containers during winter against moderate to severe frosts, since the bulbs are not so well protected as those planted in the ground.**

All in all bulbs are great value – for both colour and money – and easy to care for. Look after them well and they will reward you year after year with their beautiful shapes and colours. Planting in containers gives you the opportunity to experiment, change things around and add colour just where and when it is needed. Just plant up some pots this autumn, with tulips, daffodils, crocus and all your favourite bulbs. Next spring your patio will look as pretty as these pictures!

George developed a love of gardening from an early age. After a career in finance, he then purchased the 140 year old leading bulb company, P. de Jager and Sons Limited. I was delighted when he began appearing on QVC, bringing his wonderful bulbs to a wider audience.

Best Crops

Grow your own! There's nothing quite like the pleasure of harvesting your home grown sun ripened strawberries or tangy flavour packed tomatoes.

They're easy to grow in pots, as Matthew explains in more detail on pages 116–121. There are so many superb varieties you can grow, but here are some of my absolute favourites.

Fruit

Apples and Pears: For top cropping, choose an apple grafted onto a MM106 rootstock and grow in large pots in the sun. Regular pruning will keep it around 1.8m/6ft high. Most apple trees need another compatible apple tree or a crab apple nearby for cross pollination or grow a family tree instead. **'Falstaff'**, **'Fiesta'** and **'Sunset'** are superb varieties. Some pears such as **'Concorde'** are self fertile. Grown on a Quince C rootstock, they'll reach 1.8m/6ft or so. For really compact spaces, grow cordon apples and pears.

Peaches: Peaches need a warm, sheltered spot to do well. Over the past few years, breeders have introduced some superb naturally dwarf forms which don't reach more than 1.2m/4ft. The advantage of these is that they are small enough to be brought inside from Jan–May to help the plant avoid the cold and to prevent peach leaf curl. For top crops, pollinate the flowers with a small brush. **'Bonanza'** and **'Garden Lady'** are good choices.

Blueberries: Perfect for containers! They produce good crops for years, have pretty white, scented flowers and their leaves have brilliant autumn colour. Grow in 30cm/12in pots initially, then pot on as the plants get bigger. Use John Innes Ericaceous compost and water with rain water if possible. Blueberries are self fertile but you'll get a better crop if you grow two different varieties. **'North Sky'** grows 30cm/12in, others like **'Legacy'** and **'Liberty'** grow at least three times that size.

Oranges and Lemons: Grown outside in a sunny spot in the summer and given frost protection in winter (minimum 10°C/50°F), these evergreens are wonderful plants for the patio as they are almost always in flower or fruit. Grow in John Innes Ericaceous compost and feed all year round (Flower Power in summer and Citrus winter feed in the winter). The **calamondin orange** is naturally dwarf and bushy, while for bigger containers **'Meyer's Lemon'** is particularly good. Use my Plant Invigorator as the environmentally safe way to keep citrus pests at bay.

Strawberries: The most popular container grown fruit – they're easy, pretty and you can get great crops in pots, baskets, window-boxes and grow bags. Give them a sunny spot and keep them well watered and fed with Flower Power from the start of growth in the spring until the end of August. Remove any runners as they appear and replace the plants (and compost) after two years as they run out of steam. Summer cropping **'Loran'** and Aug–Oct cropping **'Malling Opel'** are especially good.

Peach 'Bonanza'

Calamondin oranges

Blueberries

Strawberry 'Loran'

Vegetables

Beans: Fresh picked, they taste far better than anything the supermarket has to offer. Dwarf French beans reach just 45cm/18in, grow four plants in a 30cm/12in pot or 10 in a grow bag. **'Laguna'** is an excellent variety. Runner beans are best in half barrels, grow them up a 1.8m/6ft wigwam of canes or in a grow bag against a sunny fence or trellis. Look for **'Wisley Magic'** or rose pink flowered **'Celebration'**. Keep beans well watered and fed, and pick them while young for best quality and flavour.

Lettuce: Probably the easiest salad crop to grow in containers. The pretty loose-leaf (salad bowl) like **'Lettony'** and Cos varieties, such as **'Little Gem'** or **'Frisco'**, are the best, either singly in 12.5cm/5in pots or twelve to a grow bag. Plants are readily available from garden centres, but it's easy to grow from seed in April or May. Keep well watered. The loose-leaf varieties can be picked, a few leaves at a time, over a long period.

Peppers and Aubergines: Both need sunny, sheltered spots to do well and are best grown in a greenhouse in colder areas. Grow one plant per 25cm/10in pot or three to a grow bag. Pinch out the top when they reach 30cm/12in to encourage bushier growth. Regular feeding is important. Use a high potash food like Flower Power or liquid tomato food. Just one plant of Chilli peppers will produce a huge crop (try **'Demon Red'**). For Sweet peppers, grow **'Gourmet'** and for mini-Aubergines, **'Ophelia'** or **'Orlando'**.

Beans 'Wisley Magic'

Lettuce 'Frisco'

Chilli pepper 'Demon Red'

Aubergine 'Orlando'

A planter specially made for growing potatoes.

Potatoes: Produce good crops with very little effort. Plant the tubers in as large and as deep a container as possible (having said that, I've grown decent crops in old plastic shopping bags). Plant the tubers in spring, placing them on a 10cm/4in layer of compost and cover with a further 8cm/3in layer of compost. As the shoots grow, keep covering with more compost until they reach the top of the container. Water and feed well. Try **'Charlotte'** or **'Lady Christl'**.

Tomatoes: There's nothing to match the flavour (and aroma) of home grown tomatoes. There are two types. Cordon varieties (**'Orkado'** or **'Sweet Baby'**) should be grown on 1.5m/5ft canes, all sideshoots removed and the top pinched out when the fourth truss of fruit is setting. Bush varieties (like **'Losetto'**) are easier as they are quicker to fruit and need no support or pinching out. For a hanging basket, grow **'Tumbling Tom Red'**. Grow in sun and keep well watered and fed with Flower Power.

Herbs

Bay: A handsome evergreen that can get huge in the garden, but in pots it's much more restrained and can easily be clipped to keep it in check. It needs a sunny, sheltered position and is slightly tender (many unprotected plants, sadly including mine, were lost in the recent winters) so cover with horticultural fleece if severe frosts are forecast. Trained plants (usually pyramids or lollipops) should be clipped twice a year, in mid spring and late summer.

Basil: An increasingly popular herb and an essential ingredient for many Italian dishes, this highly aromatic herb (30cm/12in) does especially well in pots (12.5cm/5in is ideal) in a warm, sheltered spot. It's a tender annual, so don't put it outside until well into June when the nights are warm. In colder areas it will do better on a sunny windowsill indoors. Pinch it out regularly to encourage bushy growth, and keep it on the dry side. For best flavour, pick the leaves as the plants come into flower.

Tomato 'Losetto'

Tomato 'Tumbling Tom'

Apple mint

Thyme

Mint: One of the toughest perennial herbs, mint is very invasive, so is best grown in pots on its own, in sun or part shade. Keep the compost moist at all times – place saucers under the pot in summer and keep them topped up with water. Apple mint has soft grey-green leaves and wonderful flavour, and the white variegated form is even prettier. Spearmint (45cm/18in) is probably the best for cooking and general all round use.

Rosemary: A fine evergreen but slightly tender so may need some winter protection in colder areas. Plant in spring, in 30cm/12in containers, so it can get established in a sunny, sheltered position over summer. Pick it regularly to keep it neat, but it does eventually become woody and will need replacing every few years. The tall, elegant **'Miss Jessopp's Upright'** grows to 1.2m/4ft while 'Severn Sea' reaches 1m/3ft. Low growing **'Prostratus'** is just 15cm/6in but less hardy.

Sage and Thyme: Two sun loving favourites. Plain green sage (45cm/18in) is the best known but the gold variegated and purple leaved forms are much prettier and look wonderful grown on their own or in mixed plantings. Trim lightly in July after flowering. Thyme forms neat evergreen mounds (25cm/10in). Common thyme has the best flavour. Grow in 20cm/8in pots and trim after flowering. For winter colour and fragrance, small pots of thyme are invaluable, especially the golden forms.

My Favourite Crops

Matthew Biggs – *Garden Writer and Broadcaster*

One of the most exciting adventures in gardening is growing crops in pots; lack of space certainly isn't a problem, all you have to do is choose the right plants and a fascinating world of freshness and flavour is yours! Don't grow veg like parsnips and Brussels sprouts, that take months to mature, it's far better to choose fast growing varieties, like lettuce and spinach using varieties you would sow in spring. Be patient with fruit – it takes a while to produce good crops but the rewards are sensational. It's the same with herbs, keep a few of your favourites on the go and you'll never want to taste dried herbs again!

My Personal Choice

Patio or dwarf varieties are excellent, if you want top crops from a single tree – help the bees and guarantee a good crop by transferring pollen from one flower to another with a soft artists paintbrush. You can do this with strawberries, too.

Apricot 'Aprigold': Large, tasty fruits on a small, tree. Wonderful blossom in April, fabulous fruit in July!

Apple 'Garden Sun Red': Sweet and juicy fruit, more of a bush than a tree!

Cherry 'Sunburst': Succulent and delicious, so glossy you can almost see your reflection in the skin! Top of my list – you never forget the first time you eat it. 5.45pm, St Anne's, Nottingham, 2009!

Lemon 'Quatre Saison's' ('Four Season's'): Reliable, producing flowers and fruit all year round. Needs winter protection.

Fig 'Rouge de Bordeau': This fig has pride of place in my garden because the fruit is so mouth wateringly delicious!

Raspberries: You can grow single raspberries up bamboo tripods in pots. I've been growing **'Tulameen'** this way for several years and it crops really well – the fruit is delicious, too!

Blueberries: These need a free draining ericaceous compost. **'Sunshine Blue'** is about 1m tall, and perfect for pots. I harvest masses from my single plant of **'Bluecrop'** but you'll get loads more with two (or three!) bushes!

Strawberries: Most strawberry pots are too small and better for growing herbs. Grow bags are ideal. **'Florence'** tastes as delicious as it looks; **'Honeyoye'** is totally reliable.

Cherry 'Sunburst'

Fig 'Rouge de Bordeau'

Strawberry 'Honeyoye'

Raspberry 'Tulameen'

My Favourite Vegetables

Carrot: **'Mokum'** is small enough for window boxes, they're sweet, ideal for juicing and taste absolutely delicious.

Aubergine: **'Baby Rosanna'** produces small fruits the size of golf balls and is ideal as a patio plant. **'Moneymaker'** is a real whopper, when it comes to fruit – and very tasty, too!

Courgette: **'Parthenon'** – Even one plant crops really well; it is great for early and late season crops. One of my favourites!

Lettuce: You can't beat **'Little Gem'** and **'Chartwell'** is tasty as well.

Spring Onions: **'White Lisbon'** is unbeatable and doesn't mind the cold.

Runner Bean: **'Hestia'** is a compact, non climbing variety, it grows happily in containers and crops surprisingly well.

French Bean: **'Purple Queen'** adds colour to containers with its flowers and purple pods. I love it!

Spinach: I've grown lots of **'Mediana'** and am sure that you'll like it, too. Pick the leaves when they're young and tender.

Beetroot: **'Bolthardy'** is a good cropper and totally reliable. **'Pablo'**, is ideal for picking when small and definitely my favourite!

Peas: **'Kelvedon Wonder'** a dwarf sweet tasting pea; **'Sugar Snap'** for pods or peas.

Aubergine 'Baby Rosanna'

Runner bean 'Hestia'

Peas 'Sugar Snap'

Beetroot 'Bolthardy'

My Favourite Herbs

Coriander: Eat the leaves before flowering for the best flavour. Its seeds are surprisingly tasty.

Mint: **'Chocolate'** mint is my favourite, but look out for Ginger, Basil, Banana and a host of other flavours.

Parsley: Needs a rich, moisture retaining compost; grow from seed every year. Pick regularly to encourage young growth.

Basil: Needs a hot sunny spot, comes in lots of different flavours from Lemon to Anise. It's worth trying them all!

Tarragon: **'French tarragon'** is far more refined than 'Russian tarragon', which is to be avoided. Perfect mild flavour for chicken dishes.

Try growing a collection of herbs in baskets by the kitchen door for easy access.

My Growing Tips

❀ Don't put small plants straight into a large pot, start them off in a small pot and move them into larger pots as they grow.

❀ **Small pots dry out really quickly in summer; those with narrow bases are more likely to be blown over!**

❀ Large containers should be moved to their final position before being filled with compost; not the other way round!

❀ **If you feel creative, want to recycle or to keep costs down, there's a real chance to have fun (right). Wooden boxes, like wine boxes, are good for growing carrots or herbs, plastic wastepaper bins suit long rooted carrots, old food cans or even thoroughly cleaned paint tins are useful, carefully file away sharp edges.**

❀ Make sure that the container is large enough. Grow runner beans in a half barrel, potatoes – especially 'early' varieties like **'Wilja'** and **'Charlotte'** in plastic dustbins or potato bags.

❀ **If you don't have the time or space to grow plants from seed buy 'plug' or small plants in modules – there's a great range available especially from mail order suppliers.**

❀ Feed plants regularly with general fertiliser – flowering and fruiting plants need a high potash fertiliser like Richard's Flower Power.

❀ **Root crops like beetroot are sweeter if eaten when they're the size of golf balls.**

❀ Water basil before mid-day, it doesn't like going to bed with 'wet feet'.

❀ **Coriander needs plenty of TLC – it must be warm, moist and draught free or it rapidly runs to seed. You can always sow the seeds or use them as flavouring!**

❀ Sow parsley when days are warm and nights are cold, as fluctuating temperatures encourage germination.

There's no doubt that fresh ingredients increase your eating pleasure; everything is so full of flavour when it comes straight from the plant to the pot – you really can taste the difference – and they're full of health giving goodness, too! Crops, like peas and carrots are so tasty they won't even reach the kitchen! Growing your own is a great chance to get the best from your favourite herbs, fruit and vegetables. Now you can experience the pleasures of kitchen gardening and of the finest ingredients.

Matthew is one of my best gardening friends. I love his wonderful passion for plants nurtured whilst he worked at Kew Gardens. Since then, he's presented highly rated TV programmes, written books, hosted garden cruises and been a popular panelist on 'Gardener's Question Time'.

Best Perennials

These are the plants that save you time and money because they provide colour and impact for years.

Some, like box, are shapely evergreens that provide style and structure all year round, others like camellias, are flowering plants and, for a few short weeks, transform the patio with a breathtaking display of colour.

Shrubs

Box: With its dense cover of small, evergreen leaves, box is ideal for clipping into globes, pyramids or spirals. It's a cracking plant for any container in sun or part shade. I especially love the topiary forms in handsome pots either side of a doorway. When buying, check out the DIY stores, they tend to have regular offers on topiary box. The best way to keep box plants in shape is to trim little and often.

Camellia: Spectacular spring flowering shrubs (up to 3m/10ft) that also have beautiful glossy evergreen leaves that make an excellent backdrop for other plants. Three of the loveliest are bright red **'Freedom Bell'**, rich pink peony flowered **'Anticipation'** and pure white, fully double **'Commander Mulroy'**. Plant in John Innes Ericaceous compost and keep well fed and watered. Lack of water, especially in late summer, causes bud drop in spring. Trim any wayward shoots after flowering.

Euonymus: Pretty evergreens with small, variegated leaves, thriving in sun or shade. **'Emerald 'n' Gold'** is low growing, with green and gold leaves that take on a pink tinge in winter. The slightly less vigorous but just as striking **'Silver Queen'** is white variegated. Both grow to 60cm/1ft. The very compact **'Microphyllus'** varieties make excellent centrepieces for winter baskets and boxes. Can be treated as a small climber if given a frame or support to grow on.

Lavender: Much loved for their aromatic silver grey leaves and beautiful midsummer flowers, lavenders are superb in containers and make a good background for other plants, especially roses. English Lavenders are much more winter hardy than French varieties. **'Ashdown Forest'** is a fine, bushy plant with beautiful pale purple flowers (50cm/20in) while the slightly taller **'Melissa Lilac'** is slightly darker but just as choice. Grow in sun and cut back hard just after flowering to keep it bushy and neat.

Skimmia: Valuable evergreens for sun or shade, with clusters of creamy white flowers in spring and, if it's a female plant, bright red berries in the autumn. **'Veitchii'** is the best for berries but it must be grown near a male variety like **'Rubella'** which has gorgeous pink-budded fragrant flowers. Both grow to 60cm/2ft. The smaller **'Reevesiana'** is self fertile but lacks the impact of the other two. For best results grow in John Innes Ericaceous compost.

Box

Euonymous 'Emerald 'n' Gold'

Camellia 'Anticipation'

Lavender 'Melissa Lilac'

Climbers

Clematis: See Raymond Evison's recommendations on page 128.

Hedera (Ivy): Tough, evergreen self clinging climbers (also grown as trailers) for sun or shade. Plant in pots at least 25cm/10in wide. The slowest growing are the small leaved forms like silver and white **'Glacier'**, gold variegated **'Goldheart'** and **'Buttercup'**, a beautiful butter gold that colours best in sun. For larger leaves, but a restrained habit, gold variegated **'Sulphur Heart'** is outstanding. Ultimate heights from 1.8m/6ft to 4.8m/16ft.

Lonicera (Honeysuckle): Beautifully scented, and tough, growing up to 3m/10ft in tubs at least 40cm/16in in diameter. For sunny spots, plant the very free flowering maroon and cream **'Serotina'**, white and yellow **'Halliana'** or the outstanding **'Graham Thomas'** with deliciously fragrant white and yellow flowers from mid to late summer. Prune back hard every spring to encourage fresh young growth.

Pyracantha (Firethorn): An easy to grow evergreen wall shrub for sun or shade, with white flowers in early summer followed by colourful autumn berries. Good in containers at least 40cm/16in wide. 'Mohave' is one of the finest: disease resistant, with heavy crops of orange-red berries, to 1.8m/6ft. If you fancy red berries grow **'Watereri'**. For yellow berries **'Soleil d'Or'**. Trim after flowering if you want to keep them neat, and watch out for those sharp thorns!

Roses: I've suggested some beauties on page 139. See also Michael Marriott's favourites on page 140.

Hedera 'Glacier'

Hedera 'Sulphur Heart'

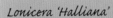
Lonicera 'Serotina'

Lonicera 'Halliana'

Pyracantha 'Soleil d'Or'

"For sunny spots plant the very free flowering maroon and cream 'Serotina'."

Sweet Peas (and other annuals): For colour, scent and cut flowers, I love Sweet Peas. And they grow fast too! I like to grow them up a wigwam of canes in a half barrel in a sunny spot. Keep them well watered and well fed, and keep picking them, as this encourages even more flowers. Varieties such as **'Cupid'** are ideal for hanging baskets but make sure they don't dry out. Other great fast growing annual plants for pyramids of colour are **Morning Glory** and **Black-eyed Susan**.

Wisteria: This classic climber for a sunny position needs a big pot (45cm/18in) or half barrel, in which the less rampant forms like **'Amethyst Falls'** reach around 3.6m/12ft. They need a strong support to grow onto and regular pruning, twice a year, for prolific flowering. In July cut the long whippy side-shoots back to within 15cm/6in of the main stem and prune these back even further, to two buds from the main stem, in February. Wisterias also look amazing grown as mop head standards in huge patio pots.

> **"For colour, scent and cut flowers, I love Sweet Peas. And they grow fast too!"**

Sweet Peas

Morning Glory

Black-eyed Susan

Wisteria sinensis trained on a circular wire frame.

My Favourite Clematis

RAYMOND EVISON – *Guernsey Clematis Nursery*

Growing Clematis in containers is incredibly rewarding and will give you so much pleasure over a long period of time. It's not a new idea, Victorian gardeners would grow them in pots outside and then bring them indoors when they flowered. They used traditional varieties which have a limited flowering period, nowadays we have a far better, longer flowering selection that have been especially bred for growing in containers.

My Personal Choice

For the smaller garden where space is limited I immediately recommend the Evison® & Poulsen® Boulevard® Collection. This group of clematis flower for most months from May until September, perhaps sleeping a little in the very hot summer time, but then flowering again once the temperature drops.

These superb clematis grow only 1–1.2m/3–4ft, they are repeat flowering and provide a range of flower colours. The flowers are about 9–15cm/4–6in in diameter but are produced in great abundance. These clematis are much more compact in their habit than the older varieties and are easier to grow and produce more flowers over a longer period of time. So they produce the most impact in a smaller space. The best of this group are:

* **c. Angelique™** – dusky pale blue flowers;
* **c. Cezanne™** – blue, ideal for sun or shade;
* **c. Picardy™** – reddish purple flowers, great in full sun;
* **c. Ooh La La™** – pink flowers and is marvellous for a shaded patio area with its bright flowers;
* **c. Chantilly™** – pale pinkish/cream which is also great for a shady part of the garden;
* **c. Fleuri™** – deep purple, brilliant in full sun;
* **c. Parisienne™** – mid-blue and a red centre which does well in any position.

If you've more space, you can get an even more colourful display by growing the taller and slightly larger flowered bright red **c. Rebecca™**, the strong blue **c. Kingfisher™**, the off-white **c. Ice Blue™**. These outstanding clematis grow to only about 1.8m/6ft and are repeat flowering. Almost all summer from May until September. Ice Blue blooms even longer. All are exceptional value.

My Growing Tips

* Choose a big container size, the larger the better, but at least 45x45cm/18x18in. It must have plenty of drainage holes at the bottom and it's important to cover these with lots of drainage material at the bottom as clematis hate cold wet feet during the winter.

* **Clematis like cool roots and grow better in ceramic, terracotta or half barrel containers rather than plastic pots which can heat up too much in the summer.**

* All of these clematis benefit from a shady root system and a good way to provide this shade is to underplant with a shallow rooted hardy perennials such as Alchemilla mollis or heathers. Alternatively, use summer or winter bedding plants to give added interest and you can change the planting combination

Clematis Angelique™

Clematis Picardy™

Clematis Cezanne™

Clematis Chantilly™

Clematis Fleuri™

Clematis Ooh La La™

Clematis Parisienne™

each year. I particularly like pastel coloured flowers or grey foliage which, I find, blend perfectly with the colours of these beautiful clematis.

❀ **If you are growing these clematis in patio containers you should select metal or perhaps willow tripods/ wigwams to support the growth of your clematis. Birch branches look lovely too.**

❀ The ideal compost is John Innes No. 3 mixed 50/50 with a multi-purpose compost. Watering is vital, especially during late spring and the summer months. Do not allow the compost to dry out this will reduce the growth and flowers that your clematis produces.

❀ **Feeding is also vital, use Flower Power or a rose fertiliser from spring until late August.**

❀ Pruning can be complicated for some clematis, but not these. Towards the end of the winter (normally late Feb/early March) chop off all their top growth down to just 15cm/6in above soil level. I call this the 'Pony Tail Cut', it is easy to do and easy to remember, but must be done each year and then you will always have the best looking, and the best flowering clematis.

I hope you have great pleasure growing them.

Clematis Parisienne™

Raymond has bred some of the world's best new clematis. His Guernsey Clematis Nursery produces annually 20% of the world's young clematis plants. He has also done wonderful work for the RHS, where he is a vice-President, who awarded him gardening's highest honour, the Victoria Medal of Horticulture.

Hardy Perennials

Ajuga (Bugle): Wonderful edging plants, forming low mats of year round colour in containers and baskets. With pretty, often variegated leaves and short (15cm/6in) spikes of blue flowers in spring, they're happiest kept well watered in sun or shade. **'Rainbow'** is an attractive mix of cream and pink, **'Braunherz'** a fine purple-bronze, **'Catlins Giant'** has fine blue flowers, and the large leaved, dark green **'Jungle Beauty'** is especially striking for winter baskets (8cm/3in)

Garden Pinks: Amazing, tough plants that can bloom all summer, producing masses of enchanting flowers (that are great for cutting). Many varieties are incredibly fragrant. Carolyn Whetman once showed me a one year old dwarf pink in a 24cm/10in pot with 300 flowers on it. The fragrance and colour was breathtaking! Grow in sun in well drained compost, height varies from 13cm/5in up. Carolyn suggests **'Whatfield Can-Can'**, **'Coconut Sundae'** and **'Raspberry Sundae'** for masses of blooms and heady fragrance.

Hellebores: These are the plants to cheer you through late winter to spring. The white Christmas rose ('Niger') is trickier to grow, so try the lovely Lenten roses ('Orientalis') with colours ranging from white through to deep plum purple (30cm/12in). I'm especially fond of the **'Ellen'** hybrids, especially the mouth-watering double flowered forms (35cm/14in). Superb in shade. Trim off the old leaves in late autumn to show off emerging flowers better and get rid of any lurking pests and diseases.

Ajuga 'Braunherz'

Garden Pink 'Whatfield Can-Can'

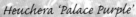

Hellebore 'Ellen'

Heuchera 'Palace Purple'

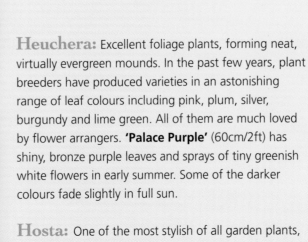

Heuchera: Excellent foliage plants, forming neat, virtually evergreen mounds. In the past few years, plant breeders have produced varieties in an astonishing range of leaf colours including pink, plum, silver, burgundy and lime green. All of them are much loved by flower arrangers. **'Palace Purple'** (60cm/2ft) has shiny, bronze purple leaves and sprays of tiny greenish white flowers in early summer. Some of the darker colours fade slightly in full sun.

Hosta: One of the most stylish of all garden plants, hostas look superb in containers especially as they begin to mature and create wonderful sculptural mounds of leaves. The flowers are incidental, but a very pretty bonus. Plant blue leaved hostas such as **'Big Daddy'** in deep shade as sunlight will scorch their leaves. **'Sum and Substance'** has bright yellow leaves in sun or chartreuse green in shade, **'Patriot'** is the best white edged variety (55cm/22in).

Hosta 'Big Daddy'

My Favourite Perennials

CLAIRE AUSTIN – *Claire Austin Hardy Plants*

Perennials are plants that come back year after year so they are ideal for anyone who has less time or money to spend on the garden. Virtually any perennial can be grown in a container, but I think that the best ones are those that produce lots of flowers or handsome leaves. Almost all perennials can be grown in sunny parts of the garden, but lots of varieties will also grow in the difficult shady areas. Another major advantage is that perennials tend to be more drought tolerant than many annual plants when grown in containers.

My Personal Choice

Bergenias: I love perennials with attractive evergreen leaves, especially those varieties which can grow in sun or shade. These include Bergenias (Elephants Ears) with large, waxy, evergreen leaves that grow into a dense clump and turn a lovely colour in autumn. In spring clusters of bell shaped flowers emerge on the top of short, thick stems. I particularly like **'Overture'** with deep pink flowers and **'Baby Doll'** with soft pink flowers.

Ajuga (Bugle): Another useful evergreen plant for either sun or shade is Ajuga. This low, spreading plant with attractively coloured leaves is ideal for growing with other plants. As it grows the long, leafy stems will spill over the sides of the pot to soften the edges. Ajugas produce short stems of tiny blue, white or pink flowers in spring. My favourite variety is **'Catlin's Giant'** with deep blue flowers and shiny, dark leaves.

Hemerocallis 'Pardon Me'

Ajuga 'Caitlin's Giant'

Eryisimum 'Bowles Mauve'

Hemerocallis: Another favourite plant is the daylily (Hemerocallis). Tough and tolerant they thrive in sun or shade and produce long stems of beautiful, trumpet shaped flowers, one or two opening every day for many months. There are lots of varieties to choose from but the best ones for pots are those that have small flowers. In my opinion one of the best is **'Pardon Me'** that produces a continuous flower of small, rich red flowers from mid June until September. Another lovely plant is **'Ed Murray'** with velvety, deep red blooms.

Eryisimum: If you want long flowering perennials look no further than Perennial Wallflowers (Erysimum). These are easy to grow and produce clusters of gently scented, small, flat flowers for many months. Ones to choose include **'Bowles Mauve'** with pretty bluish purple flowers and **'Constant Cheer'** with dusky orange flowers that become purple with age.

Verbena: For something a little different try **Verbena bonariensis**. A butterfly attracting plant, the slender, stiffly upright stems are topped with flat heads of small, soft purple flowers from June until October. If placed behind other pots this lovely plant provides an airy see-through effect for many months.

Hostas: On the theme of handsome foliage it would be difficult to miss out Hostas. These large leaved plants are decorative from the moment they emerge in early spring until the first frosts arrive in autumn. Hostas can also be left in a pot, undisturbed, for many years. I have a wonderful specimen of Hosta **'Patriot'** with oval, white edged, deep green leaves that has been in the same pot for over 5 years.

Hosta 'Sum & Substance'

Hosta 'Krossa Regal'

Hosta 'Patriot'

Hosta **'Sum and Substance'** with yellow leaves and **'Krossa Regal'** with grey leaves are also excellent varieties. All hostas can be grown in sun (although some varieties may get scorched in direct sunlight) they are even better when grown in the shade. Also, if you grow hostas in pots, slugs are far less likely to graze on them, especially if the pot is sitting on gravel.

My Growing Tips

✿ Whichever perennial you choose, as they are long lived and may take a year or so to reach full size, it is advisable to grow them in a soil-based compost in a container that is twice the size of the initial root ball.

✿ **In autumn and spring give the pot a light feeding of a good all-round fertilizer.**

✿ Generally very few pests attack perennials, but it wise to gently tip the plant out of the pot each year to check for vine weevil grubs, which love to feed on plant roots.

Perennials really are easy-to-grow plants, providing pretty flowers and lush foliage throughout the growing season. Just put them in the pot (you can also include a few colourful annuals too), water frequently but not excessively and watch them come back year after year.

Claire inherited her love for gardening from her father, David Austin, the world famous rose grower. She took over her father's collection of peonies, irises and perennials, started propagating them and eventually set up her highly regarded nursery. Her knowledge and enthusiasm for her plants is respected worldwide. In her spare time, she gardens and writes award winning books.

Roses

Miniatures and Patio roses: Miniature roses are exquisite. They only grow to 45cm/18in and will flower all summer. Look for bright orange/red **'Starina'** or yellow **'Rise n shine'**. Patio roses grow slightly bigger (60cm/2ft) and are my favourites. They're as good as bedding plants for summer colour yet can last up to ten years! Clip back lightly every spring to keep in shape. Grow in 30cm/12in pots that are at least 25cm/10in deep. I love peach **'Sweet Dreams'** while deep red **'Anna Ford'** and pink edged white **'Regensberg'** are also highly rated.

Ground cover roses: These are tough, free flowering and remarkably easy to grow, as long as the pot is at least 30cm/12in deep. To tidy them up, simply clip with shears in spring. Most grow to about 45cm/18in or so tall, but do tend to get much wider, spreading beyond the width of the container so they need a little space to give of their best. Top choices include brilliant magenta pink **'Berkshire'**, lavender **'Magic Carpet** (it's got a delicious spicy fragrance too!) and purple **'Gloriana'**.

Shrub roses: Most of the wonderfully romantic old shrub roses aren't suitable for containers – they get too big and most have a short period of flower. Some of the smaller varieties will grow happily in a 40cm/16in pot such as **'Little White Pet'** with masses of white pompoms, blush pink **'Cecile Brunner'** and pale apricot **'Perle d'Or'**. For the best colour, impact, fragrance and Flower Power though, grow the English roses – see Michael Marriott's recommendations on page 140.

Rosa 'Sweet Dreams'

Rosa 'Little White Pet'

Rosa 'Cecile Brunner'

Standard roses: Lovely as the centrepiece in a half barrel, underplanted with lavenders or other roses. They should always be well staked. Patio rose standards are the most suitable, and I'm very fond of the semi-weeping groundcover standards too such as **'The Fairy'**, with clusters of pale pink pompom flowers all summer. It's one of the most enchanting sights.

Climbing roses: For summer long colour, pick the repeat flowering climbers and plant them in a sunny spot in 45cm/18in wide containers that are a minimum 30cm/12in deep. Pale salmon-orange and fragrant **'Compassion'** and glorious deep red **'Dublin Bay'** grow to 3m/10ft. Smaller, but just as beautiful are the climbing miniature roses (1.8m/6ft) especially golden yellow **'Laura Ford'** and soft salmon pink **'Nice Day'**.

Rosa 'Fairy'

Rosa 'Compassion'

My Favourite Roses

MICHAEL MARRIOTT – *David Austin Roses*

Growing roses in containers is a wonderful way to display and enjoy our nation's favourite flower. Container gardening enables you to be that little bit more intimate with roses and to appreciate the blooms and the fragrances at closer quarters. Importantly, it also means that you can enjoy growing them in places where it normally would not be possible.

My Personal Choice

There is huge variety within the rose world but most groups of roses can be grown in containers. There is a rose to fit every size of pot, from the miniature in the tiny pot on the window ledge to the climber or rambler growing in a much larger one against the patio fence. Most people are probably looking for something in-between, perhaps for a paved area or for their balcony, and since scent is such an important part of a rose I always think some of the English Roses are particularly suitable. They are the most fragrant group of roses not only in strength but also in variety – Old Rose, Myrrh, Tea, Fruity and Musk.

✿ Some of the best are **'Grace'** and **'Lady Emma Hamilton'** which are both apricot; the pure rose pinks of **'Harlow Carr'** and **'The Mayflower'**; the apricot-pink **'Jubilee Celebration'** and the wonderfully dark red **'Munstead Wood'**. Each of these roses has an attractive rounded habit, which looks particularly good in a container.

✿ If you have a wall or trellis but no soil to plant anything in, a climbing rose in a pot can be a very good

Rosa 'A Shropshire Lad'

solution. The English Rose climbers with their ability to produce flowers from top to bottom are perfect; they are not too vigorous and so are easy to keep under control. Some of the best varieties are **'A Shropshire Lad'**, **'James Galway'** and **'Mortimer Sackler'** – all have few thorns and so are less likely to attack you as you walk past!

✿ For a small area you will need to choose a small rose that will fit in a correspondingly small pot, so here choose one of the Patio Roses or one of the Dwarf Polyanthas (such as **'The Fairy'** or **'Little White Pet'**). While not all that fragrant, they are very free-flowering and will give a wonderful show of brightly coloured flowers for weeks on end.

Rosa 'Munstead Wood'

Rosa 'Lady Emma Hamilton'

Rosa 'Harlow Carr'

Rosa 'Grace'

Rosa 'Mortimer Sackler'

✿ You don't have to plant just roses in containers; try mixing them with other plants, preferably ones that are not too vigorous. Some of the annuals like **'Love-in-a-Mist'** or the small Nasturtiums are very pretty, as are the many different varieties and colours of Penstemon. They not only look good with roses but they also help to attract beneficial insects that will hopefully gobble up aphids.

My Growing Tips

✿ Choose good, healthy varieties and plant them in pots that are big enough for their size. For an English Rose I would go for a pot at least 50cm/18in deep that holds at least 25 litres of compost. A climber will need a bigger pot, whilst a smaller rose will need a pot of just 10 litres or less.

✿ **I make a special 70:30 mix – 70% multi-purpose compost with 30% John Innes compost. I find this gives the roots plenty of air and the pot a bit of weight to stop it blowing over.**

✿ Generous watering is also key to their success and so remember that the smaller the pot the quicker the compost will dry out and the sooner you will have to water it again – roses are great survivors but will sulk quite badly if allowed to dry out too much.

✿ **Roses like plenty of food so feed them regularly with Flower Power or apply a long term controlled release fertiliser at the start of the season.**

The possibilities of gardening with containerised roses are endless. I urge all gardeners to have fun and experiment with them – they can be so beautiful.

Few people know more about roses than Michael! He joined David Austin Roses initially as Nursery Manager and latterly as Technical Director which means he now advises rose growers around the world. He's designed some fabulous rose gardens too, including those at Regents Park and Alnwick.

Rosa 'James Galway'

Grasses and Bamboos

Carex: Beautiful and resilient grasses, most of them evergreen that thrive in pots. **C. testacea** is a stunner (60cm/2ft), forming wonderful sprays of orange-green leaves that change hue through the season. Neil Lucas, in his superb book *Designing with Grasses* comments that its natural arching habit is even more striking in tall containers. Best in full sun and beautiful with orange flowered geums and 'Princess Irene' tulips. Neil also rates dark bronze **C. dipsacea**.

Festuca: For a modern, contemporary look, these are unbeatable. Grow these compact, neat and colourful evergreens on their own or use them as a foil for other plants. The steely blue leaved forms of **F. glauca** are fantastic, especially **'Siskiyou Blue'** and **'Elijah Blue'** (40cm/16in) and they both look amazing in sunny spots. Trim back the old growth every spring to encourage lots of fresh, brightly coloured new leaves.

> **"Grow these compact, neat and colourful evergreens on their own or use them as foils for other plants."**

Festuca glauca 'Elijah Blue'

Hakenchloea Aureoli

Pennisetum x advenia 'Rubrum'

Phyllostachys nigra

Hakenchloea: I first fell in love with this plant when I saw it growing in a pot in Adrian Bloom's glorious garden at Foggy Bottom in Bressingham, Norfolk. Adrian was growing **H. aureoli** (45cm/18in) which forms astonishing mounds of gold and green striped leaves that ripple in the gentlest of breezes. Slow growing, in shade it goes greener while in full sun it turns a brighter yellow. Keep it well watered and don't worry as I did when my plant died back in the winter, it's not an evergreen!

Pennisetum: I was introduced to these fabulous grasses by Neil Lucas from Knoll Gardens. He's *the* grass expert and considers them amongst the most beautiful of all grasses. And I agree, they are sumptuous! Neil's top recommendation is the purple fountain grass P. x advenia **'Rubrum'**, 'absolutely stunning in colour, shape and form' with deep red leaves followed by 'exquisite arching red flowers that fade to beige' (1.2m/4ft). Needs winter protection in colder areas.

Bamboos: For year round impact, these magnificent evergreens are amongst the very best. They provide height, colour and, when the breeze rustles their leaves and stems, sound and movement too. Best grown in big pots on their own and they must be kept well watered or the leaves turn brown. Use John Innes compost No. 3. Fast growing varieties need re-potting every two years, in the autumn. Look for the golden stemmed forms, and the astonishing ebony black stemmed **Phyllostachys nigra**.

Trees

Acer (Maple): The Japanese maples are all time favourites and no wonder, they've everything you want, attractive leaves, glorious autumn colour and a neat shape which even looks good in winter. Acer palmatum has fresh green, palm shaped leaves that turn deep red in autumn, **p. atropupureum** has glowing deep red leaves (1.8m/6ft). The cut leaves forms **p. dissectum** are slower growing but even prettier (1.2m/4ft). Grow in light shade, in a protected spot sheltered from strong winds and keep well watered.

Amelanchier (Snowy Mespilus):
Although it can be grown as a shrub, it can be bought as or grown into a tree. It's a beauty, with colour changing leaves which start bronze green, go green in the summer and then turn fiery orange and red in the autumn. The springtime flowers are wonderful too, with clouds of the prettiest small white flowers. It's a bit boring in summer though, so plant colourful bedding around the base, or grow a compact clematis through the branches.

Betula (Birch): Amongst the tallest of trees that will happily grow in a container, birches are especially loved for their glowing white bark. **B. pendula 'Tristis'** has elegantly drooping branches and can reach 3m/10ft or more. Dome shaped **B. pendula youngii** is a true weeper, to 2.5m/8ft. But my favourite is the upright Himalayan Birch, **jacquemontii** with glistening white bark but it can grow 4m/13ft. Some birches have whiter stems than others, so don't buy unseen. Grow in sun or partial shade.

Acer palmatum 'Atropupureum'

Amelanchier

Malus 'Evereste'

Prunus 'Kojo-no-mai'

Malus (Crab Apple): Beautiful spring blossom and a colourful autumn display of ornamental fruit. The award winning **'Evereste'** is simply wonderful, with masses of red budded white flowers, good autumn colour and shiny red fruits that last until Christmas. Highly recommended! **M. floribunda** is an attractively domed form to 3m/10ft with tiny yellow apples and the smallest of the lot is bushy **M. sargentii** (1.8m/6ft) with red flushed fruits. Grow in sun or partial shade.

Prunus (Ornamental cherries):
Spectacular in flower, but rather dull for the rest of the year, with a few exceptions. **'Kiku-shidare-zakura'** (Cheal's weeping cherry) develops into an umbrella-like weeper with pink double flowers, **'Amanogawa'** forms an upright column to 3m/10ft but my choice, the tiny, bushy **'Kojo-no-mai'** (1.2m/4ft) has pink flowers aging to white, and brilliant autumn colour. All these ornamental cherries do best in sun.

"Japanese maples are all time favourites and no wonder, they've everything you want."

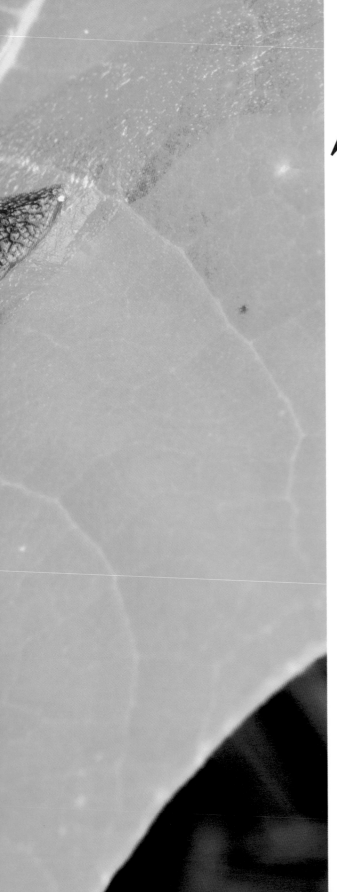

Trouble-shooting

One of the great things about container gardening is that if you water and feed your plants regularly, they should flourish. Healthy plants tend to be more resistant to diseases and pests. However, occasionally, problems may occur but if you keep an eye on your plants (which isn't difficult if you're watering them regularly during the summer) you can spot early warning signs and nip it in the bud before it becomes a major problem. With any luck, you won't need to consult this section at all, but just in case, here's my potted guide to the most common problems you might come across.

Pests

Slugs and Snails

The number one pest, the little blighters get everywhere, they even manage to find their way into hanging baskets. The telltale signs are holes eaten in leaves and, often, a slime trail is also visible.

Prevention: Mulch containers with washed, sharp gravel or moisture absorbing granules such a Westland Slug blocker granules. Or place a copper band around the pot, the slimy molluscs won't travel over it.

Cure: Use a biological control, microscopic slug (but not snail) killing nematodes such as Nemasys. Or apply my environmentally friendly, pet and wildlife safe Slug and Snail control pellets (which are also approved for organic growing).

Vine Weevil

The creamy white, brown headed grubs live in the compost, eat the roots of the plant which subsequently wilts, discolours, then collapses and dies. The adult beetles are grey/black with speckled gold and eat irregular shaped notches in the edge of leaves.

Prevention: If you see any grubs when potting up, squash them. And get rid of the adult beetles too by treading on them. Use a thick mulch of sharp grit or gravel (2cm/0.75in deep) to prevent the female laying eggs in the compost.

Cure: Use a biological control like Nemasys Vine Weevil Killer or water on a chemical control such as Provado Vine Weevil Killer 2 but, at the time of writing, this can only be used on ornamentals so check the label to see if it has approval for edible crops too.

slugs

Vine weevil

Greenfly

Lily Beetle

Greenfly and Blackfly

Sap sucking insects that attack a wide range of plants, feeding on stems, buds and flowers which may become distorted. Often the leaves have a sticky coating too.

Prevention: If you see early signs of an attack, pinch out the affected shoot (and bin or burn it) or simply wipe off any small infestation with your fingers.

Cure: Spray with my environmentally friendly, non-toxic Plant Invigorator which also kills many other pests on contact. Alternatively pick one of the many chemical insecticides sold by garden centres and DIY stores like Scotts Bug Clear for Fruit and Vegetables. When you spray, don't forget the undersides of the leaves, that's often where they hide (and lay their eggs).

Lily Beetle

The bright red beetles eat holes in the leaves and flowers of lilies (as well as other plants in the lily family). The entire plant can be stripped bare in a matter of days. The other telltale sign is a black, gungy deposit on the stems and leaves which covers (and hides) the beetle larva.

Prevention: Squash the beetle on sight.

Cure: Spray the bugs and grubs with my Plant Invigorator which kills on contact or use the chemical Provado Ultimate Bug Killer which provides a few weeks protection from one spray application.

Diseases

Downy Mildew

Yellowing, discoloured leaves with white patches beneath. It's most common after a prolonged wet spell, particularly when plants are very close together. The plants die slowly through the summer. This disease has become a major concern with busy lizzies in the past year or so.

Prevention: A few varieties of lettuce and other crops are resistant to the disease so choose them if possible. Currently there aren't any disease resistant busy lizzies so grow begonias instead or Sunpatiens. If the disease does occur, try to limit the spread by removing then binning or burning the affected leaves.

Cure: There are no chemicals available at the moment that can be used by home gardeners.

Powdery Mildew

This is one of the most common diseases to affect container plants and most often occurs in warm, dry weather especially if you've not been watering as often as you should. A powdery white coating appears on the upper surface of the leaves and they eventually turn yellow and fall off.

Prevention: Pick off any affected leaves and spray with my Plant Invigorator (surprising I know, but this is what many commercial growers do). Keep the containers well watered.

Cure: Spray a fungicide such as Bayer Garden Systhane on the young leaves.

Powdery mildew

Holiday care

Grey Mould

This is more of a problem in wet seasons. Yellow or brown patches appear on leaves, stems and flowers, followed by greyish white fuzzy fungal growth, then rotting.

Prevention: Pick off any affected material as soon as you spot it. Improve air circulation around the plant and remove any old material (like faded flowers) regularly.

Cure: There aren't any chemical controls for grey mould at the moment.

Holiday Care

When I was the gardening correspondent for the *News of the World*, a reader once wrote to me to say that he always worried about his pots and baskets whilst he was on holiday. So he solved the problem by taking them on holiday with him!

There are simpler ways. If possible ask a neighbour to pop in and water them regularly. If you're going to be away for more than a week, push your luck slightly, see if they would feed them as well. Don't worry about any deadheading, that can wait until you get back.

If you don't want to ask your neighbours, you could just move all your containers into a cool, shady spot (do this a few days before you go to fox any would be burglars), water them thoroughly just before you set off and most plants will survive very happily for a week.

If you're going away for longer, then you could pop a bottle top watering spike in each container (see page 30) or use an Aquapod system with a watering timer.

Index

Acknowledgements

This book is dedicated to the marvellous team at QVC. Thank you to all of them for introducing so many people to the enjoyment of gardening.

I'm extremely grateful to many people who have helped me with this book: **Angela Noghani**, **Martin Chaplin** and **David Hawkins**, all of whom encouraged me to write a follow up to my 150 tips book.

The experts who have very kindly contributed their special sections: **Claire Austin, Matthew Biggs, George Clowes, Raymond Evison, Paul Hansord, Michael Marriott** and **David Ponton**. Thanks also to **Bob Willard** and **Geoff Hodge** from De Jager for their additional contribution. A number of gardeners have also generously advised me whilst I was writing the best plants section, including **Stuart Wassell** and **Stuart Lowen** (Ball Colegrave); **Sarah Curtis** and **Wayne Eady** (Delamores); **Paul Hansord, Michael Perry** and **Colin Randel** (Thompson & Morgan). The photographic credits follow on, but I'd like to especially thank **Julie Butler, Anna Collingwood, Paul Cooper, Sarah Dodsworth, Rob Emmanuel, Tom Gamon, Gary Heany, Val Jackson, Mal Keen, Joanna Oldham, Dan Whiting, Chris Waterlow** and **Kevin Wood** for their help taking and sourcing many of the pictures.

Above all, a huge thank you to my designer, **Arthur Brown**, who has done such a fantastic job in creating this beautiful book.

Finally, I'd like to thank my family, **Val, Chris, Nick** and **Sarah**, for their good humoured support and also for watering all those pots and baskets every time I was away!

The Raymond Evison clematis featured in this book have official plant breeder registrations:
c. Angelique™Evipo017(N), c. Cezanne™Evipo023(N),
c. Picardy™Evipo024(N), c. Ooh La La™Evipo041(N),
c.Chantilly™Evipo021(N), c. Fleuri™Evipo 042(N),
c. Parisienne™Evipo019(N), c. Rebecca™Evipo016(N),
c. Kingfisher™Evipo037(N) and c. Ice Blue™Evipo003(N).

Picture Credits

Key: l (left); r (right); c (centre); t (top); b (bottom); all (all photos on that page or range of pages).

Andrew Lawson: 16b; **Burgon & Ball:** 20r; **Claire Austin Hardy Plants:** 134–137all; **Clive Nichols:** 1, 12l, 19t, 71, 119t, 119bl, 123bl, 145b, 147t, 147; **David Austin Roses:** 140–143all; **Dave King:** 14–15, 26–27all, 28r, 28l, 53, 55t, 55b, 104; **Fairweather's Nursery:** 102t, 123br; **Graham Strong:** 19b, 38r, 39, 47t, 48b, 50, 51, 60, 62r, 65, 66b, 73, 77c, 77r, 111tr, 127bl, 127r, 132t, 150t; **Hayloft Plants:** Simon Fletcher 75–76all (colour wheel illustrations), 77l, Derek Jarman 78tl; **Hozelock:** 31, 153; **Jessica Biggs:** 121br; **Jill Brown:** 48t; **John Glover:** 20t, 28l, 35, 42l, 63r, 70, 72, 107tl, 108, 109t, 111br, 115t, 115b, 117tr, 117br, 124t, 124b, 125tl, 125br, 125r, 144b, 145t, 151t, 152; **Marianne Majerus Garden Images:** Heather Edwards 43, 45t; Andrew Lawson 91b, 107tc; Marianne Majerus front jacket, back jacket (designers Susan Bennett and Earl Hyde), 2, 4, 6–7 (design Bowles & Wyer), 10–11, 12r (designer Jon Baillie), 13r (designer Marty Hoffmann), 17 (designers Susan Bennett and Earl Hyde), 18 (RHS Garden, Wisley), 20b, 23l, 23r (designer Pattie Barron), 24 (Lowder Mill), 34 (The Old Vicarage, East Ruston, Norfolk), 40–41, 42r, 45b (designer Kathy Brown), 46, 49, 62l, 64, 66t (designer Julie Floyd), 68–69 (Vann, Surrey), 78–79, 101b, 102t, 119br (designer Kathy Brown), 120t, 120–121b, 121tr, 123tl, 126, 146t, 146b, 148–149; **P. de Jager & Sons Ltd:** 74, 96–100all, 101t, 105tr, 107bl, 107tr, 107cr, 107br, 109br; **QVC:** Rob Emmanuel 155, Gary Heany 9, Chris Waterlow 156, 160; **Raymond J. Evison:** 128–131all; **R. Delamore Ltd:** 80, 81br, 86t; **Richard and Val Jackson:** 16t, 25t, 25b, 30b, 32, 33, 36r, 38l, 54, 56, 59t, 59b, 67, 90b, 102b, 105l, 155, 156, 159, 160; **Shutterstock:** Mark Bridger 150b; Adam J. Sablich 151b; **Thompson & Morgan:** 47b, 80–85all, 86b, 87–88all, 89t, 89b, 90t, 91t, 92–94all, 95b, 111tl, 11bl, 112–113all, 114t, 114b, 117tl, 117bl, 118t, 118b, 127t, 144t; **Tom Gamon:** 30t, 36l, 57, 58; **Whetman's Pinks:** 132b.

> "I've been happily gardening for over 40 years and during that time, I've worked with many professional nurseries and groundsmen. Part of the secret of their success is using specially formulated products. Frustrated that these products weren't readily available to home gardeners, I developed my own professional formula range. I'm very proud of my products. I use them and get great results and, more importantly, so do many other gardeners, from beginners to experts."

For more details on these and all of my products, visit:

www.richardjacksonsgarden.co.uk

Happy gardening!